D0906024

Eating Disorders

Other Books of Related Interest:

Opposing Viewpoints Series

Feminism

Interventions

Nutrition

Self-Mutilation

Teenage Sexuality

At Issue Series

Alcohol Abuse

Can Diets Be Harmful?

How Does Advertising Impact Teen Behavior?

Current Controversies Series

Alternative Therapies

The Global Impact of Social Media

Vegetarianism

"Congress shall make no law . . . abridging the freedom of speech, or of the press."

First Amendment to the US Constitution

The basic foundation of our democracy is the First Amendment guarantee of freedom of expression. The Opposing Viewpoints series is dedicated to the concept of this basic freedom and the idea that it is more important to practice it than to enshrine it.

OPPOSING VIEWPOINTS® SERIES

Eating Disorders

Roman Espejo, Book Editor

GREENHAVEN PRESS
A part of Gale, Cengage Learning

GALE
CENGAGE Learning·

Detroit • New York • San Francisco • New Haven, Conn • Waterville, Maine • London

GALE
CENGAGE Learning·

Christine Nasso, *Publisher*
Elizabeth Des Chenes, *Managing Editor*

© 2012 Greenhaven Press, a part of Gale, Cengage Learning.

Gale and Greenhaven Press are registered trademarks used herein under license.

For more information, contact:
Greenhaven Press
27500 Drake Rd.
Farmington Hills, MI 48331-3535
Or you can visit our Internet site at gale.cengage.com

For product information and technology assistance, contact us at

Gale Customer Support, 1-800-877-4253
For permission to use material from this text or product, submit all requests online at
www.cengage.com/permissions

Further permissions questions can be emailed to permissionrequest@cengage.com

Articles in Greenhaven Press anthologies are often edited for length to meet page requirements. In addition, original titles of these works are changed to clearly present the main thesis and to explicitly indicate the author's opinion. Every effort is made to ensure that Greenhaven Press accurately reflects the original intent of the authors. Every effort has been made to trace the owners of copyrighted material.

Cover Image copyright © 3dMedical.com/Corbis.

LIBRARY OF CONGRESS CATALOGING-IN-PUBLICATION DATA

Eating Disorders / Roman Espejo, book editor.
    p. cm. -- (Opposing viewpoints) Summary: "Eating Disorders: Are Eating Disorders a Serious Problem?; What Causes Eating Disorders?; What Role Does the Internet Play in Eating Disorders?; How Should Eating Disorders Be Treated?"-- Provided by publisher.
    Includes bibliographical references and index.
    ISBN 978-0-7377-5723-1 (hardcover) -- ISBN 978-0-7377-5724-8 (paperback)
    1. Eating Disorders--Juvenile literature. I. Espejo, Roman, 1977-
    RC552.E18E28211217 2012
    616.85'26--dc23
                                                                2011037074

Printed in the United States of America
2 3 4 5 6   16 15 14 13 12

FD094

Contents

Why Consider Opposing Viewpoints?   11

Introduction   14

Chapter 1: Are Eating Disorders a Serious Problem?

Chapter Preface   18

1. Eating Disorders Are a Growing Threat   20
   to Public Health
   Senate Committee on Health, Education,
   Labor and Pensions

2. The Threat of Eating Disorders Is Distorted   26
   Malcolm Evans

3. Eating Disorders Are a Growing Problem   32
   Among African American Women
   Tedra Coakley

4. Eating Disorders Are a Growing Problem   42
   Among Asian American Women
   Elaine Low

5. Binge Eating Disorder Is Linked to Obesity   49
   and Other Health Problems
   Sara Selis

6. The Obesity Epidemic Is a Myth That   59
   Promotes Unhealthy Weight Loss
   Linda Bacon

Periodical and Internet Sources Bibliography   66

Chapter 2: What Causes Eating Disorders?

Chapter Preface   68

1. Genetics Play a Significant Role   **70**
   in Eating Disorders
   Johanna S. Kandel

2. Genetics May Not Play a Significant Role   **76**
   in Eating Disorders
   Simona Giordano

3. Cultural Obsession with Thinness Is Harmful   **82**
   Michelle M. Lelwica

4. Some Perceptions of Thinness Are Unfair   **88**
   and Harmful
   Julia Cheng

5. The Fashion Industry Promotes Eating Disorders   **93**
   Jessica Bennett

6. The Fashion Industry Should Not Be Held   **100**
   Responsible for Eating Disorders
   Lisa Hilton

7. Binge Eating Is Linked to Genetic   **107**
   and Environmental Factors
   Cynthia M. Bulik

Periodical and Internet Sources Bibliography   **116**

**Chapter 3: What Role Does the Internet
Play in Eating Disorders?**

Chapter Preface   **118**

1. Pro-Ana Websites Are Dangerous   **120**
   Lauren Cox

2. Some Eating Disorders Websites Offer Support   **127**
   Jaclyn Gallucci

3. Thinspiration Videos Are Misguided Attempts   **140**
   at Artistic Expression
   Virginia Heffernan

4. Pro-Ana Websites Should Be Regulated   146
   Royal College of Psychiatrists

5. Pro-Ana Websites Should Not Be Regulated   152
   Adam Thierer

Periodical and Internet Sources Bibliography   157

Chapter 4: How Should Eating Disorders Be Treated?

Chapter Preface   159

1. Involuntary Treatment for Anorexia Is Justified   161
   Cornelia Thiels

2. Involuntary Treatment for Anorexia May   171
   Not Be Justified in Some Cases
   Avis Rumney

3. Family Therapy Is an Effective Treatment   177
   for Anorexia
   Julie Deardorff

4. Acceptance and Commitment Therapy Is an   185
   Effective Treatment for Eating Disorders
   Kathy Kater

5. Antidepressants Are Effective in the Treatment   191
   of Bulimia
   Michael J. Gitlin

6. A Structured Eating Plan Can Control   197
   Binge Eating
   Jane E. Brody

Periodical and Internet Sources Bibliography   203

For Further Discussion   204

Organizations to Contact   207

Bibliography of Books   212

Index   215

Why Consider Opposing Viewpoints?

"The only way in which a human being can make some approach to knowing the whole of a subject is by hearing what can be said about it by persons of every variety of opinion and studying all modes in which it can be looked at by every character of mind. No wise man ever acquired his wisdom in any mode but this."

John Stuart Mill

In our media-intensive culture it is not difficult to find differing opinions. Thousands of newspapers and magazines and dozens of radio and television talk shows resound with differing points of view. The difficulty lies in deciding which opinion to agree with and which "experts" seem the most credible. The more inundated we become with differing opinions and claims, the more essential it is to hone critical reading and thinking skills to evaluate these ideas. Opposing Viewpoints books address this problem directly by presenting stimulating debates that can be used to enhance and teach these skills. The varied opinions contained in each book examine many different aspects of a single issue. While examining these conveniently edited opposing views, readers can develop critical thinking skills such as the ability to compare and contrast authors' credibility, facts, argumentation styles, use of persuasive techniques, and other stylistic tools. In short, the Opposing Viewpoints Series is an ideal way to attain the higher-level thinking and reading skills so essential in a culture of diverse and contradictory opinions.

In addition to providing a tool for critical thinking, Opposing Viewpoints books challenge readers to question their own strongly held opinions and assumptions. Most people form their opinions on the basis of upbringing, peer pressure, and personal, cultural, or professional bias. By reading carefully balanced opposing views, readers must directly confront new ideas as well as the opinions of those with whom they disagree. This is not simplistically to argue that everyone who reads opposing views will—or should—change his or her opinion. Instead, the series enhances readers' understanding of their own views by encouraging confrontation with opposing ideas. Careful examination of others' views can lead to the readers' understanding of the logical inconsistencies in their own opinions, perspective on why they hold an opinion, and the consideration of the possibility that their opinion requires further evaluation.

Evaluating Other Opinions

To ensure that this type of examination occurs, Opposing Viewpoints books present all types of opinions. Prominent spokespeople on different sides of each issue as well as well-known professionals from many disciplines challenge the reader. An additional goal of the series is to provide a forum for other, less known, or even unpopular viewpoints. The opinion of an ordinary person who has had to make the decision to cut off life support from a terminally ill relative, for example, may be just as valuable and provide just as much insight as a medical ethicist's professional opinion. The editors have two additional purposes in including these less known views. One, the editors encourage readers to respect others' opinions—even when not enhanced by professional credibility. It is only by reading or listening to and objectively evaluating others' ideas that one can determine whether they are worthy of consideration. Two, the inclusion of such viewpoints encourages the important critical thinking skill of objectively evaluating an author's credentials and bias. This evaluation will illuminate an author's reasons for taking a particular stance on an issue and will aid in readers' evaluation of the author's ideas.

It is our hope that these books will give readers a deeper understanding of the issues debated and an appreciation of the complexity of even seemingly simple issues when good and honest people disagree. This awareness is particularly important in a democratic society such as ours in which people enter into public debate to determine the common good. Those with whom one disagrees should not be regarded as enemies but rather as people whose views deserve careful examination and may shed light on one's own.

Thomas Jefferson once said that "difference of opinion leads to inquiry, and inquiry to truth." Jefferson, a broadly educated man, argued that "if a nation expects to be ignorant and free . . . it expects what never was and never will be." As individuals and as a nation, it is imperative that we consider the opinions of others and examine them with skill and discernment. The Opposing Viewpoints series is intended to help readers achieve this goal.

David L. Bender and Bruno Leone,
Founders

Introduction

"Men with eating disorders have been overlooked."

—*Arnold Andersen,*
psychiatrist and coauthor of
Making Weight: Men's Conflicts with
Food, Weight, Shape & Appearance

In 2010 a former model with anorexia nervosa died at thirty-eight years old, weighing only sixty-six pounds at five feet eight inches tall. That the sufferer was male, Jeremy Gillitzer of Minneapolis, Minnesota, was just as shocking to those unfamiliar with his story. Three years earlier, Gillitzer posed bare-chested for the cover of *City Pages*. Not for a fashion spread—his ravaged, pale torso and limbs resembling nothing of his formerly muscular, tan physique—but for a feature on him as an anorexic male. In fact, it was not under the pressures of modeling that Gillitzer starved himself and feverishly exercised. As a teenager, he had been hospitalized for anorexia, and, in 2004, he relapsed after a series of stressful events: the end of a long-term relationship with his partner, his mother's illness, and two automobile accidents. "The actual act of purging relieves anxiety—physiologically, it's one of the things it does," Gillitzer told *City Pages* in a November 2007 interview. To connect with other men suffering like him, Gillitzer started blogging about his illness, sometimes in unsparing detail. "I am hunchbacked because my muscles cannot support my neck. I am extremely constipated. I have a bedsore on my tailbone from the friction. An 80-year-old lady, you ask? No, a 35-year-old man," he posted on his blog in June 2007.

Anorexia has long been associated with women and girls. They represent the majority of cases, but emerging research claims that men and boys like Jeremy Gillitzer are not an anomaly, but an unnoticed group that faces eating disorders. In a 2007 study of three thousand adults, researchers at Harvard University found that 25 percent of individuals with anorexia or bulimia are male. "These disorders are less common in men, but maybe not quite as rare as we once thought," James I. Hudson, lead author of the study, stated in *City Pages* in November 2007. Some men, for instance, face rigorous weight restrictions in numerous sports or the military that may lead to unhealthy dieting and weight loss. Furthermore, according to a 2009 report published by the Agency for Healthcare Research and Quality, hospitalizations for eating disorders from 1999 to 2006 increased 119 percent among patients age twelve and younger, including a significant number of boys. "The younger you get, the more likely they are to be boys," insisted David Rosen, the lead author of the report, in an article on CNN.com in December 2010. "For the youngest patients, we see roughly equal number of boys and girls." And while the influence of the fashion industry on anorexia and body image is under debate, the ideal male body, as seen on runways and in advertising campaigns, has shifted from athletic to the waifish thinness of their female counterparts. "Far from inspiring a spate of industry breast-beating, as occurred after the international news media got hold of the deaths of two young female models who died from eating disorders, the trend favoring very skinny male models has been accepted as a matter of course," *New York Times* fashion critic Guy Trebay explained.

What is different, some experts point out, is how the sexes show the telling signs of anorexia. Instead of an ideal weight, men and boys tend to fixate on achieving or maintaining a toned or muscled appearance at the expense of body fat. "Boys say, 'I'm getting into shape,' not, 'I'm fat and gross and need to go on a diet,'" stated Adelaide Robb, associate professor of psychiatry at George Washington University School of Medicine and Health Sciences, in a March 2007 article in the *Wash-*

ington Post. For instance, Robb explained that a teenage son's change from calorie-laden junk food to diet-conscious fare may be viewed as positive by parents. "They often think he's adopted healthy eating habits," she added. Others suggest that they are less likely to come forward with anorexia because it is perceived as a woman's disorder and fear being stigmatized. "Never once did I say 'anorexia' aloud during high school," recalled writer Snowden Wright, who weighed seventy-six pounds at age fourteen during the worst part of his illness. "I was horrified what it would say about me, to have a 'girl's disease.' I worried what people would think," he explained in *Salon.*

Other estimates for anorexic males, nonetheless, are more conservative, with 10–15 percent of individuals with anorexia or bulimia the commonly accepted figure. But its prevalence in other groups, especially minority women, is under increased investigation. *Opposing Viewpoints: Eating Disorders* explores this and other issues in the following chapters: Are Eating Disorders a Serious Problem?, What Causes Eating Disorders?, What Role Does the Internet Play in Eating Disorders?, and How Should Eating Disorders Be Treated? From the onset of anorexia and bulimia to methods of treatment, the authors' conflicting views underline the controversies and unknowns surrounding eating disorders.

OPPOSING VIEWPOINTS® SERIES

CHAPTER 1

Are Eating Disorders a Serious Problem?

Chapter Preface

Selective eating disorder (SED) has received increased attention in recent years. According to Great Ormond Street Hospital for Children (GOSH) in the United Kingdom, it "is characterised by eating a very narrow range of foods usually for a number of years, together with a reluctance or refusal to try new foods." It is normal for toddlers and young children to be picky eaters. "However for some young people the problem persists into middle childhood, adolescence and even adulthood. So whilst most children will grow out of it, a small number do need help to change their eating behaviour," states GOSH. Foods deemed "unsafe" by those suffering from SED are usually rejected because of their smell, texture, or color.

SED is not formally recognized in adults; it may be added to the next version of the *Diagnostic and Statistical Manual of Mental Disorders* in 2013. Sufferers of the disorder, however, insist that it negatively affects their quality of life. Heather Hill of North Carolina, who never dines with her children and eats only about seven kinds of foods, said in a July 2010 article in the *Wall Street Journal*, "When I was younger it was cute. Now it's embarrassing." Also, some experts maintain that the potential for health risks are high. "If you are an adult picky eater, there is a good chance you may not be getting balanced nutrition," claims Fran Berkoff, a dietitian and nutrition columnist. "If you are specifically leaving out something like protein, say, and you don't know how to get it other than from the meat you've chosen not to eat, your diet could be problematic." Others, however, contend that SED does not apply to all cases of food pickiness. "[M]y food preferences do not impinge on my life anymore and are borne more out of habit and whimsy, leading me to conclude that although I eat pickily, I am not an official picky eater," asserts British journalist Lucy McDonald, who eschews a long list of foods.

In the following chapter, the authors probe the severity and scope of eating disorders.

"Eating disorders wreak havoc on a person's psyche and body."

Eating Disorders Are a Growing Threat to Public Health

Senate Committee on Health, Education, Labor and Pensions

In the following viewpoint, testimony before the US Senate Committee on Health, Education, Labor and Pensions, it is argued that eating disorders are a growing threat to the public. Eating disorders are commonly associated with major psychological issues and can lead to medical complications. The testimony contends that there is a major need for access to care for those suffering from eating disorders.

As you read, consider the following questions:

1. According to the viewpoint, which eating disorder has the "highest mortality rate of all the psychiatric disorders"?

Senate Committee on Health, Education, Labor and Pensions, "Testimony of the Eating Disorders Coalition for Research, Policy & Action: Hearing on Women's Health," *The Promoting Healthy Eating Behaviors in Youth Act of 2002 as part of a Women's Omnibus Health Bill*, April 25, 2002. Reproduced by permission.

2. As stated in the viewpoint, women with anorexia are how many times more likely to die than other women without an eating disorder?

3. According to the viewpoint, do insurers ignore the standard of care for eating disorders?

Eating disorders though not uncommon, especially among women, continue to go unrecognized as an important health priority, and are often overlooked entirely in national health campaigns such as the Healthy People 2000. Until Congress addresses eating disorders through research, treatment and prevention, more young people will suffer and die unnecessarily. The amendment promoting healthy eating as a way to prevent eating disorders and other health problems is an important step in recognizing eating disorders as a public health threat in need of policy attention.

Eating Disorders as a Public Health Threat

Eating disorders are a growing public health threat with an estimated 8 million Americans suffering from eating disorders. Eating disorders cut across race, color, gender and socioeconomic categories. No one is immune. Eating disorders wreak havoc on a person's psyche and body. They are commonly associated with substantial psychological problems, including depression, substance abuse, and all too frequently with suicide. They also can lead to major medical complications, including cardiac arrhythmia, cognitive impairment, osteoporosis, infertility, and most seriously death. Anorexia nervosa has the highest mortality rate of all the psychiatric disorders. A young woman with anorexia is 12 times more likely to die than other women her age without anorexia. The frequency of suicide is 75 times greater than expected in young women without eating disorders.

The Need for Access to Care

The challenges for people with eating disorders accessing appropriate treatment have created a lethal situation. We receive calls practically every week from those suffering from eating disorders, their families or friends seeking help accessing treatment. Just this week [in April 2002] we received a call about a 15-year-old girl in the hospital with severe anorexia weighing only 55 pounds and being fed through tubes—whose health insurance company refused her coverage because anorexia is a mental disorder not a physical disease. Last week we received a call from a young woman in a residential treatment center who was panic-stricken, as she was told that her insurance company would not pay for her treatment. In her darkest hour, when she is already feeling defeated and unworthy, she is forced to fight for the care she so desperately needs. The week prior to this we received two such calls.

Health insurance companies contribute to the high death rate by either denying care or limiting the number of days they will reimburse for treatment. Research shows that eating disorders can be successfully overcome with adequate and appropriate treatment. Yet such treatments are typically extensive and long term. The practice of insurance companies routinely limiting the number of days they will reimburse forces doctors to discharge patients with anorexia nervosa too early. Although patients with eating disorders typically require more than 6 weeks of inpatient therapy, hospitalization or residential treatment for proper recovery, insurance companies offer an average of 10–15 days a year. Typically insurers completely ignore the standards of care for eating disorders established by the American Psychiatric Association [APA] and published in the APA journal in 2000.

According to a survey of eating disorder specialists conducted in conjunction with ANAD [the National Association of Anorexia Nervosa and Associated Disorders], 100% said that their patients are suffering relapses as a consequence of

The Changing Face of Eating Disorders

Globalization allows Western culture to export many products and ideas. Unfortunately, for global girls, part of this legacy promotes a relationship to food and to the body that takes away more than it gives and puts their lives at risk.

For many years, eating disorders were found almost exclusively in highly industrialized Western nations like the United States, Canada, and some western European countries. Other cultures seemed immune to them. As globalization proceeds, however, this pattern has changed dramatically. Now the list of nearly 40 countries reporting eating disorders includes places as unexpected as Nigeria, India, China, South Korea, South Africa, the former Soviet Union, and Mexico. Yet there is a common factor among these seemingly disparate countries: Each, in its own way, has begun to idealize thinness in women. In contrast, eating disorders simply do not appear in cultures that reflect more reasonable body-image norms.

Margo Maine,
Father Hunger: Fathers, Daughters,
and the Pursuit of Thinness.
Carlsbad, CA: Gürze Books, 2004.

such managed care coverage limits. And virtually all specialists believed that patients with anorexia are placed in life-threatening situations because their health insurance policies mandate early discharge.

Passing the mental health parity bill for those with eating disorders is a matter of life and death. The longer Congress waits, the more young people we will lose. We urge Congress to pass this bill with haste.

Important Role of Prevention

In addition to pushing for treatment for those currently suffering from eating disorders, it is equally important to offer prevention programs for youth. Primary efforts are designed to prevent the occurrence of eating disorders before they begin by promoting healthy development.

Experts on optimal prevention programs for eating disorders conclude that successful programs are designed to promote healthy development, thus are multidimensional and comprehensive. Successful curricula include not only information about nutritional content but also information about responding to hunger and satiety, positive body image development, positive self-esteem development, and learning life skills, such as stress management, communication skills, problem-solving and decision-making skills. Successful interventions are tailored to the developmental and cultural needs of the target population and include family, school and community involvement. . . .

The Dire Need for Prevention Research Dollars

If we do not begin widespread, well-researched, effective eating disorder prevention programs to foster healthy eating habits in youth, the costs to our society and to our health care system will be devastating. As many as 5–10% of people with anorexia nervosa or bulimia nervosa will die prematurely—many struck down in the prime of their lives. Even those who recover suffer needlessly, impairing their intellectual, academic, vocational, economic, social, emotional and personal functioning. Furthermore, countless women of all ages and increasing numbers of men also suffer from subclinical eating disorders, demonstrating some, but not all, of the symptoms of eating disorders. As they are unlikely to receive treatment, their compromised nutritional intake can lead to serious health problems such as cardiac irregularities, chronic gastrointestinal disorders, infertility, osteoporosis, as well as severe anxiety and mood fluctuations.

The lack of substantial funding for prevention-oriented research is one of the greatest problems contributing to the ongoing increase in eating disorders and related conditions. The research done to date has begun to differentiate effective prevention approaches from ineffective ones. We desperately need more funding to build on this body of knowledge and begin to eradicate these life-destroying illnesses. The EDC [Eating Disorders Coalition for Research, Policy and Action] urges the committee to move this important women's health bill forward.

> *"At a time when the most extreme phase of eating disorders in the West appears to be over, the definitions of what can constitute an eating disorder becomes more open."*

The Threat of Eating Disorders Is Distorted

Malcolm Evans

Malcolm Evans is founder and secretary of the Weight Foundation, a British charity that researches dieting and eating disorders. In the following viewpoint, Evans contends that the definitions of eating disorders have become too flexible in a culture preoccupied with obesity and weight loss. Today, anyone who has problems with body image and dieting, he claims, can easily qualify as suffering from an eating disorder. In fact, obsessive dieting has been normalized, and individuals use anorexia and bulimia as ways to identify with others and to feel a sense of belonging, the author states.

As you read, consider the following questions:

1. How did dieting change in the 1980s and 1990s, in Evans's opinion?

2. How does the author compare unrealistic images of thin women to the need to fit it?

3. What is the author's recommendation for children and eating?

Increasingly, we are running the risk of projecting our own food paranoia on to our children, while at the same time conveniently ignoring our own demons.

In the West we are stitched culturally into a food-centric mentality as tightly as a haggis is squeezed into its skin. Cultural and commercial pressures conspire to keep us there, and the quality of political debate is far from savoury.

The nanny state has been getting up quite a head of steam over the past year or so. This 'Slimming by Statute' movement points its accusing finger at the usual bogeymen—big business, in this case the leviathans of the international food industry. Even better should they be American: the likes of McDonald's and Coca-Cola stand accused of seducing us into obesity.

And the Right has its equally simplistic counterpoint. In their flurry of opinion pieces, right-wing commentators argue that only stupid, weak, selfish people get overweight (unless, like some authors, of course, they are sufficiently sassy and independently minded that they can choose to be overweight). The loathsome mass-market fatties are the new objects of ridicule, even the new enemy within. Opprobrium has moved on from the chavs to the fatties, whatever the reality and implications of the so-called 'obesity epidemic' itself.

So people feel obliged to do something. At the governmental level we get a slew of vacuous worthiness. The US and Britain have been making aspirational announcements for over 100 years about the 'ideal diet' for their citizens. Down to the present day the public generally pays not a blind bit of notice to such exhortations, unsupported as they are by any excitement of hard sell from the diet industry.

And this is where all the action remains. For many long-term dieters it has ceased to have much to do with weight loss and has simply become a badge of ongoing food-related distress and confusion. It's a Dantesque horror, hopping from one futile fad diet to the next with no end to the torment in sight.

Dieting Has Gone Mainstream

It's gone mainstream, it's going more hardcore, and it's getting them younger. Dieting started for those who could afford to be precious about food back in the Victorian era but it only really took off in the 1960s. It was a rebel thing women flirted with in their twenties when they left home—they picked at their food but they didn't starve.

But by the 1970s they certainly did starve, as anorexia blossomed alongside Women's Lib and the explosive growth of the dieting industry.

By the 1980s dieting was becoming just a way of life, with the rarely mentioned and rather unpleasant side effect of growing armies of women privately putting two fingers up to it all in the form of booming bulimia. By the mid to late 1990s the cult of superwomen had moved on a bit and the ideal continues to be the average athlete who can juggle career, home, kids and weight distress.

These days the West is increasingly exporting its more extreme anorexia and bulimia to second-world countries and settling back into a comfortable and predictable phase of endemic eating dysfunctionality.

It has crept gradually down the age scale over the past 40 years, from the mid-twenties in the 1960s, on to mainstream teenage fashion and, by the 1990s, to the preteen audience. It then hit a problem: that of children being below the age of dieting understanding and hence dieting consent. But hardcore dieting is nothing if not ingenious in its expansionism and so it did something very clever—it got the mothers to take it right back to age zero, skipping the awkward years in between.

Mothers increasingly prefer 'formula' milk and prepackaged infant food because you can carry on the counting obsession. Forget the vagueness of some lightly steamed vegetables mashed up with a little minced or flaked fish—you know exactly where you are with labels. This is the highest achievement to date of the creeping process of nutritional dislocation which is paralysing natural feeding instincts.

It would strike one as utterly absurd if there was a whole industry and national obsession premised on uncertainty and quack advice about breathing. Yet this is how we have become regarding eating. For several millennia people have managed quite well feeding themselves.

Surprisingly Elastic

It gets worse, as it is all being clouded over by a justification that says this is merely a concern with 'eating disorders.' Just as it is remarkable how few poor people have genuine food allergies, so can the definitions and claims surrounding eating disorders become surprisingly elastic. Some people can die from the merest fraction of a peanut, and death by anorexia is a cruel torment—but the great unspoken in all of this is often the surrounding disingenuous whimsicality.

At a time when the most extreme phase of eating disorders in the West appears to be over, the definitions of what can constitute an eating disorder becomes more open. One only needs to cast around a selection of eating disorder websites to bear this out. Most people who have ongoing doubts about self-image and have any significant history of failed dieting can walk straight into the eating disorders camp. Illness is a third-party treatment issue; pathologisation is a lockout to self-help.

The keys to unpacking and unpicking the nutrition conundrum need not be overly complex, nor the preserve of medical specialists. Many commentators now recognise that commercial dieting is the reddest of herrings with regard to lasting and relaxed weight control and is in fact a major contributory factor to widespread obesity.

To some extent it is one of those 'white bear' things, whereby the more you try not to think about something the more it dominates your consciousness. A practical step is to loosen the three restricting bands which keep food and dieting fixations in place.

Ignoring any one of the emotional, cultural or commercial pressures will almost certainly condemn a problem eater to weight-control failure.

Food, Not Mood

Apart from occasional celebration and a backdrop to sociability, eating needs to be food, not mood. Less widely appreciated than the unrealism of waif-thin icons is the need women especially feel to be involved with dieting—the need to fit in with friends and society by talking, living and suffering it. Hardcore dieting has sadly become for many a rite of passage into womanhood.

Similarly, men are increasingly under pressure to hop on the body beautiful bandwagon; manhood could be the next major eating battleground.

Good nutrition needs to be a background and enabling environment, not a constantly in-your-face (often literally) obsession. Mind-shifts do not occur in the stomach. Kids should not be made doppelgangers to their parents' eating hang-ups, but rather be allowed to mature naturally out of their puppy fat.

[Poet] Philip Larkin might just as well have been referring to food when he wrote of parents, 'They fill you with the faults they had and add some extra, just for you.' Today, when parents' and adult society's attitudes to food remain raw and unrefined, the future doesn't look especially rosy for our children.

> *"Researchers and therapists have indicated that now, minority women are just as likely as white women to develop an eating disorder."*

Eating Disorders Are a Growing Problem Among African American Women

Tedra Coakley

Despite curvier ideals of beauty in black communities, Tedra Coakley asserts in the following viewpoint that anorexia, bulimia, and binge eating are on the rise among African American women. Also, physicians and therapists often assume that these minority women do not experience eating disorders, insists Coakley, due to the stereotype that only middle- and upper-class Caucasian women suffer from them. The author recommends that treatment and support groups expand and reach out to women of diverse backgrounds. Based in Columbia, South Carolina, Coakley works in public relations and is a former magazine editor.

Tedra Coakley, "Eating Disorders No Longer Discriminate," *Inner City Conservative Journal*, December 20, 2007. Reproduced by permission.

As you read, consider the following questions:

1. As described in the viewpoint, what methods are African American women more likely to use to control their weight than Caucasian women?

2. What undermines African American women's greater appreciation for their bodies and curves, in Coakley's opinion?

3. What is happening to images of minority women as the media diversifies, in Coakley's view?

Many Americans have had high standards when it comes to weight, but now, it seems to be turning into an obsession.

And if that's not bad enough, the media have discovered and exploited this. There are references to weight all over television, radio, print, and the Internet. It may seem that much of the media are just feeding the needs of Americans, but, in retrospect, they are feeding a disease that consumes more and more Americans every day.

"Black people don't have eating disorders," said Beatrice Heyward, a 22-year-old African-American from Charleston, S.C.

That's what many African-Americans believe when it comes to eating disorders. A middle- or upper-class white female is the stereotypical media image of an individual with an eating disorder. But, recently, reports of eating disorders in women of color have increased and are continuing to rise. Researchers and therapists have indicated that now, minority women are just as likely as white women to develop an eating disorder.

"I think that we're right behind Caucasians or No. 1," says Whitney Tucker, 21, a nursing major at Hampton University. Stress and "not embracing our body type," are two of the causes she mentions.

Defining Eating Disorders

There are three types of eating disorders: anorexia nervosa, bulimia nervosa and binge eating disorder, explained the Web site, www.healthline.com.

- Anorexia is a psychological disease that is characterized by a distortion of body image and an obsessive fear of weight gain.

- Bulimia is characterized by compulsive eating followed by deliberate purging, the use of laxatives or excessive exercise in order to prevent weight gain.

- Binge eating, which resembles bulimia, is characterized by eating excessive amounts of food at one time until one is physically uncomfortable. Binge eating differs from bulimia in that there is an absence of purging.

The Facts

In the PBS documentary "Dying to Be Thin," on *NOVA*, which aired on Dec. 12, 2000, Drs. Marian L. Fitzgibbon and Melinda R. Stolley of the Department of Psychiatry and Behavioral Sciences at Northwestern University's medical school, said that bulimia and binge eating are more common than anorexia.

Fitzgibbon and Stolley have also found that standard rates in females with bulimia are 1 to 3 percent and one half percent for those with anorexia. Binge eating ranges from 5 to 8 percent in obese individuals in communities.

In a Sept. 20, 2005, article from the *New York Times*, Ruth Striegel-Moore, professor and chairwoman of the Psychology Department at Wesleyan University, said, "Minority women are not getting treated. It's very clear from my studies that black American women do experience eating disorders, but doctors and therapists still operate under the assumption that they don't; therefore, they aren't prepared to deal with them clinically."

Gayle Brooks, an African-American psychologist specializing in eating disorders at the Renfrew Center in Coconut Creek, Fla., said that because medical experts believed that minorities were "immune" to developing an eating disorder, there have not been a lot of studies conducted on them. In the past, most studies have focused on white females.

"More attention should be paid to minorities as well so in the future they can diagnose them right," said Anahita Tipnis, a 20-year-old Asian-Indian from Charleston, S.C.

According to the South Carolina Department of Mental Health, out of all mental illnesses, people with eating disorders have the highest mortality rate. In an article published in *Essence* magazine on Jan. 1, 1994, it was reported that 53.5 percent of their respondents, who were black females, are at risk for developing an eating disorder.

The January 2000 *Archives of Family Medicine*, vol. 9, says that black females are more likely to control their weight through fasting and the use of laxatives and/or diuretics than white females. According to Striegel-Moore, they are also as likely to report binge eating as whites.

African-Americans and the Media

Traditionally, African-American females have been thought to have some protection against eating disorders because of a greater acceptance of larger body size in the African-American community, says Brooks.

Many black women have a greater appreciation for their bodies and having curves is something that is celebrated in the black community, says Shannette Harris, an associate professor of clinical psychology at the University of Rhode Island.

But as American media exploit America's obsession with weight and glorify youth and appearance, black women feel the need to fit into that category.

Concerned with Thinness

Similar to their white counterparts, as black girls approach adolescence, they become concerned with thinness. Studies indicate that when African-American girls experience social pressure to be thin, they express the same type of body dissatisfaction and drive for thinness as white girls. Adolescents from middle-class African-American families may be particularly vulnerable to the influence of the white beauty ideal. *Essence,* a magazine that caters to African-American women, regularly runs stories on body size anxiety and eating disorders. A survey of its readers indicated that African-American women appear to have at least equal levels of abnormal eating attitudes and behaviors as white women. Studies indicate that blacks who identify with mainstream culture exhibit more eating problems, including dieting and fear of fat.

Dana K. Cassell and David H. Gleaves,
The Encyclopedia of Obesity and Eating Disorders.
New York: Facts on File, 2006.

"Americans and much of the Western world are not only obsessed with weight but with appearance in general, which feeds into the focus on the external rather than the internal qualities a person has," says Carolyn Hersh, a mental health counselor who runs a National Association of Anorexia Nervosa and Associated Disorders (ANAD) group in Norfolk, Va. "I would say that much of the media impact actually has to do with advertisers. Advertisers fuel unrealistic expectations in order to get us to buy their products. They show us what we don't have—the 'perfect' and therefore unrealistic body, or relationship, or material things—and then imply that their product will give us those things. And the assumption is that if we have those things, we will feel better about ourselves."

Some of those women believe that being thin will help them fit into mainstream America. As the media diversify, they are incorporating images of thin minorities alongside with their white counterparts.

"I think it's a terrible epidemic," says Shona Lewis, 21, a student at Hampton University from Closter, N.J. "Our African-American community is already dying down from AIDS. It's sad that they're getting caught up in eating disorders."

The Causes

We don't really know specifically what "causes" an eating disorder other than it is some combination of environment, personality, and biology, says Hersh. "Eating disorders are symptoms. They are the way that some people find to manage their issues around control, perfectionism, people-pleasing, lack of assertiveness, fear of rejection and a myriad of other things."

According to the National Eating Disorders Association (NEDA), eating disorders develop from issues stemming deeper than just food and weight. For many, eating disorders can develop in individuals who feel that they lack control in some aspect of their lives. Food becomes the only thing that they can control.

"In my opinion, it takes a whole series of events to come together to produce an anorexic child or bulimic child," says Susan Joseph, a therapist in Hampton, Va. "One of the main things is parental pressure. The anorexics I had, had these parents who were intrusive. They crossed boundaries; they were too involved in the child's life."

NEDA offers some of the social, personal and psychological factors that can lead to eating disorders.

Social:

- Cultural interpretations of beauty—most of the mainstream magazines in America, such as *Vogue* and *Cosmopolitan*, showcase unrealistic standards and body types in their models.

- Peer pressure—friends may push those unrealistic standards on you and flaunt their smaller frames.

- Non-diverse attitudes—people who only have one standard of beauty and look down on those who look different than them.

Personal:

- Physical and/or sexual abuse—could lead to low self-esteem and self-worth; negative body image.

- Ridicule from family and friends—comments and jokes about weight can lead to self-consciousness about one's body and low self-esteem issues.

- Family issues—divorce, incarceration, or death can cause stress and lack of control, which could lead one to focus on food, something they can control.

- Relationship issues—verbal abuse could lead to low self-esteem and self-worth.

Psychological:

- Stress—could lead to forgetting to eat or not wanting to eat.

- Trouble with self-esteem—could develop a distorted image of what one should look like.

- Lack of confidence—low confidence could lead to one's body image becoming skewed.

- Lack of control—some turn to food, the only thing they believe they can control.

Warning Signs

The Web site Helpguide.org names some of the warning signs and symptoms of eating disorders.

- Irritability and moodiness

- Obsessive habits

- Wearing baggy clothes

- Changes in hair, skin and nails

- Social withdrawal

- Fatigue

- Loss or irregularity of menstrual cycle

- Going to the bathroom after meals

- Hoarding food

- Rapid weight loss

Some of these can seem like normal adolescent behavior, which is why so many cases of eating disorders can go undetected. Being aware of these and other symptoms can help someone before it's too late.

Health Consequences

There are many consequences of eating disorders. If not treated, an eating disorder could lead to death, but before your body reaches that point, it can develop other problems, such as:

- Low blood pressure—due to a lower body temperature, malnutrition and dehydration.

- Osteoporosis—due to the depletion of calcium and proteins in the bones.

- Tooth decay—from stomach acids due to frequent vomiting.

- Hair loss—caused by stress due to frequent vomiting and lying about it.

- Liver damage—due to the lack of digestion, in which the liver aids.

- Dehydration—lack of fluid intake.

- Inflammation of the esophagus and ulcers—due to frequent vomiting.

- Irregular heartbeats—due to an electrolyte imbalance.

- Heart disease—due to an increase in triglyceride levels.

These and other consequences listed on NEDA's Web site can be avoided by early detection and immediate treatment.

Treatment

Many Web sites and health professionals stress that it is important to seek treatment early on. NEDA also provides information on different treatment options. Psychological counseling is the most effective in achieving long-term results. Along with that, nutritional counseling is vital in the recovery. Other forms of treatment can include support groups, family therapy and/or hospitalization, such as the Renfrew Center, which is the first residential eating disorder treatment center in the United States.

The National Association of Anorexia Nervosa and Associated Disorders (ANAD) offers 250 support groups in the United States, two in Canada and one in China.

Now that this disease is becoming more prevalent in all races and cultures, doctors and treatment centers need to do more in diagnosing and treating this problem. Support groups should also be more prevalent. Those struggling with eating disorders find it easier to deal with when they find [other] people struggling [with them] as well. Although, ANAD offers many [support groups] throughout the country, some places have more than others. For example, there are 19 groups in California, three in Virginia and none in South Carolina, which is the writer's home state.

"South Carolina has a lot of women with eating disorders too," says Ronald White, a 21-year-old from McClellanville, S.C. "Just because Hollywood or Los Angeles has a lot of celebrities doesn't mean they should have more [support groups]. South Carolina should at least implement a few for now."

While support groups aren't a substitute for treatment, it's important that these women have a sort of safe haven to go to. Aside from treatment, the media need to take their focus off of weight and appearance. As clichéd as it sounds, what's inside is more important than what's on the outside. This may be the first step in preventing the development of a potential eating disorder.

It's important for young girls and women, especially African-Americans, to know that they are not alone. Thousands of people just like them struggle with this life-threatening disease every day, but many have overcome this battle and many more will after first being honest with themselves and seeking treatment.

> *"Yet even with these [eating disorders] numbers, Asian American women in particular may often feel ignored in the national discussion."*

Eating Disorders Are a Growing Problem Among Asian American Women

Elaine Low

In the following viewpoint, Elaine Low suggests that eating disorders affect an increasing number of Asian American women. Along with pressures to conform to Western beauty standards, ideals of thinness in their own cultures influence anorexic or bulimic behaviors in this group, Low explains. However, many Asian American women are reluctant to seek treatment or even tell others about their eating disorders, she says, because of the important roles of food and negative attitudes toward mental illness in their families and communities. Based in Los Angeles, California, Low is a writer and former managing editor of Mochi, *an Asian American online magazine.*

Elaine Low, "Diagnosing the Asian American Eating Disorder," MochiMag.com, January 14, 2010. Reproduced by permission.

As you read, consider the following questions:

1. In Teresa Mok's view, what is the racial component to eating disorders in Asian American women?

2. What role does food play in Asian immigrant communities, according to Low?

3. What happens when Asian Americans underutilize mental health resources, in Low's view?

The first time Grace* forced herself to throw up, she was 19 and recovering from a painful breakup. After a long summer of calorie counting and subsisting solely on a diet of fruit, vegetables and tofu, Grace found herself "jonesing badly for pizza." That afternoon, she gave in to her craving and went on a binge she immediately regretted.

"I took the back of my toothbrush and threw up the pizza in one swooping puke," said the 5'2", 120-pound Korean American, who wears a size 2. "It was difficult to silence the gagging noise, but my parents and my brother were at home so I must have been desperate to get it out of my body."

Grace is not alone. She is one of millions of young women across America who struggle with eating disorders—an estimated one in five women have disordered eating, according to the National Institute of Mental Health, with 90 percent of those between the ages of 12 and 25. Yet even with these numbers, Asian American women in particular may often feel ignored in the national discussion.

Not Just a "White Woman's Issue"

From Kelly Taylor's diet pill abuse on *Beverly Hills, 90210* to DJ's excessive workouts on *Full House* to Blair's bulimia on *Gossip Girl*, eating disorders have traditionally been portrayed on network TV as a problem that only affects young, middle- to upper-class, Caucasian women.

* Names have been changed.

"It's meaningful that a white woman can turn on a TV and find a broad range of characters, but Asian Americans are portrayed the same way over and over again," said Dr. Teresa Mok, a clinical psychologist who treats a lot of college students. "For someone struggling with self-esteem issues, this reinforces the feeling of invisibility."

Eating disorders are often seen as a "white woman's issue," she says, a stereotype reflected in the lack of research on this topic among women of color. And interestingly, race not only ties in to how eating disorders are portrayed, but also how they develop. From the Asian American clients she sees at her private practice in Urbana, Ill., Mok discerns a common theme that lies at the root of many eating disorders, albeit subconsciously.

"It's not just about weight. There's always a racial component to it," she said. "There's a general body dissatisfaction with eye shape, hair color, breast size, nose," but, she added, "No client [overtly] says, 'I want to be white.'"

The pursuit of Western beauty ideals often plays a large role in the development of disordered eating habits, with the media subliminally urging women to want all of the aforementioned physical features—the image on most magazine covers at the checkout aisle.

Dr. Sand Chang, a clinical psychologist who teaches intercultural awareness development at the California School of Professional Psychology, said people who don't see themselves "reflected in what is seen as 'normal'" are propelled to work even harder to fit into that mold.

And that mold can be a tight fit even by Asian beauty standards, in which women stereotypically are seen as being naturally "petite," with porcelain skin and angular features. Grace, a second-generation Asian American, said she wasn't as affected by American media as much as she was by images of

Too Large to Be One of Them

I have never been a heavy person, but for some reason, my physique drives some Korean people insane. They feel that I am too large for them to be comfortable, too large to be one of them, so they go out of their way to tell me what to do about it. It is either personal weight-loss secrets or cautionary tales about people who refused to lose weight ("And she never got married . . ." followed by a shudder). If it isn't that, it is because I have lost weight and they must comment on how much better I look. Most commonly, it is to inform me that on television I look grossly overweight, but in person, I look great.

My relatives were probably the worst to me about my weight, since they had my entire life to pester me about it. My mother and father, when they'd call me on the phone, would say, "How is your weight?" instead of "Hello." It got to be so unbearable that whenever they said it, I would immediately hang up on them and not let them speak to me unless they stopped saying it.

Margaret Cho, I'm the One That I Want.
New York: Ballantine Books, 2001.

Korean pop groups with 90-pound girls. "I would be thinking, 'Wow, I'm 30 pounds overweight,' when I was a healthy 120 pounds," Grace recalls.

Stuck Between Cultures—and Classification

While mainstream American media tends to gloss over the issue of body image in minority communities, so do mainstream research methods. "Most psychological research [to date] has been done on affluent white populations, usually college populations, and a lot of the research has only looked at the two major syndromes—anorexia or bulimia," said Chang. "A lot of clinics won't even look at you if you don't meet the criteria."

Although the common perception is that eating disorders only fall into two categories, the majority of people dealing with disordered eating actually fall into a third category called EDNOS, or Eating Disorder Not Otherwise Specified, according to the current *Diagnostic and Statistical Manual of Mental Disorders*. This category would include someone who binge eats without purging or starves herself without losing her period, i.e., someone who has all the symptoms of an eating disorder minus the extreme effects.

Grace may have begun purging the summer she was 19, but she had started exercising rigorously months before that, sometimes going to the gym up to three times a day, and keeping a strict watch on her calorie intake.

"I had always been self-conscious about my body and had low self-esteem," she said. "Rather than concentrate on consuming food like I'd done the first 19 years of my life, I concentrated on *not* consuming it, and when I felt like I had lost control, I concentrated on *un*-consuming it." The step between *not* consuming and *un*-consuming is a small leap, but one that distinguishes between *not* having an eating disorder and actually qualifying for a diagnosis.

Grace said she knew she had to get help when she was "bingeing and purging four to five times a day." What she didn't know was that her behavior leading up to "full-blown" bulimia is also considered as disordered eating. As Dr. Mok asserted, "Part of the problem is that the [current] definition excludes culture, the preoccupation with food, weight, binge eating."

And food is such an integral part of Asian and Asian American culture. Particularly in immigrant communities, food *is* culture, a way to connect with unique pasts and histories. Curry, kimchi, char siu bao—these words break down the umbrella term "Asian American" into its distinct roots using nothing more than lunch dishes.

"The significance of eating or not eating has complicated meaning," said Chang. "Food is used as love. Take the image of the Asian mother saying, 'Eat, eat, eat.' Meal times are frequently the only times to connect [with family]." For someone with an eating disorder, the battle between control and culture can be as stressful as the disorder itself.

"We Have to Start Asking What's Wrong Here"

Grace, now 23, has been dealing with bulimia for "four years and counting," but had a hard time initially revealing her struggle to her strict Korean parents.

"For me, my identity as the eldest child of immigrants has everything to do with my eating disorder," she said. "Bulimia is about control. I control the amount of food I consume. I control the amount of food I purge. I abused [my eating habits] to cope with feelings I couldn't express because of cultural differences in my family."

These differences often make it difficult to talk about sensitive topics like mental health, especially in cultures that see such issues as bringing shame to the family.

"[Being] a second-generation Asian American brought about enormous amounts of pressure and an unfulfilled desire for independence," Grace said. "I wanted to make my own life decisions, but [I somehow believed] that going against my parents was a slap in their faces, as if I was turning my back on the hardships they experienced. I internalized guilt through self-destruction."

Grace finally told her parents about her bulimia—two years after her first purge—and eventually went to see a therapist. But she said the first step long before that was telling a friend, and she has since gotten a handle on her eating disorder by slowly tearing down the "wall of lies and deception that [she] had built up."

"I stopped sneaking around for my next fix of food and throwing up," she said. "I was open and honest. I wasn't ashamed to speak about my self-esteem and my relationship with food."

A psychologist can be a useful resource in preventing problems from erupting. Because Asian Americans underutilize mental health resources available to them, researchers and health administrators may be led to believe that the community doesn't need them at all, which is far from the case.

"Asian Americans tend to underreport mental health issues," said Dr. Szu-Hui Lee, a clinical psychologist and director of training at the McLean Hospital at Harvard Medical School. "There's a big stigma with seeing a psychologist. [Asian American] parents are more likely to send their kids to an academic counselor than a psychologist."

"Asian American women have one of the highest suicide rates," said Lee. "People really have to start scratching their heads and asking what's wrong here."

The key to prevention is talking about it. To those who still struggle in secret, Grace advised, "Talk to someone. It sounds easier than it is. Eating disorders make you secretive and distrustful of everyone. But choose one person that you can confide in, and at least hear someone else other than your brain that's tearing you down enough to punish your body."

> "Since binge eating is most common among the overweight and obese, those populations are the logical place to start screening."

Binge Eating Disorder Is Linked to Obesity and Other Health Problems

Sara Selis

A former health care journalist and editor, Sara Selis is a graduate student in social work at San Jose State University. In the following viewpoint, she writes that binge eating disorder (BED) is not yet recognized as a psychiatric illness, but is widespread and undertreated, especially among the overweight and obese. The author maintains that BED is associated with severe obesity as well as diabetes, heart disease, hypertension, and stroke. Nonetheless, she states, physicians have limited awareness of the disorder and do not routinely screen for it in their patients. While treatment options include cognitive behavioral therapy, medication, and self-help, Selis advises that recovery requires lasting behavioral changes.

As you read, consider the following questions:

1. How does the author characterize the incidence of BED in men?

2. Why do physicians overlook BED, in the author's opinion?

3. What distinguishes BED from overeating, as told by the author?

Though binge eating is not an officially recognized psychiatric disorder, it is more common than anorexia nervosa and bulimia; carries serious health risks; can be chronic; transcends racial, gender and socioeconomic boundaries; and frequently occurs along with other mental disorders.

Given these findings—taken from the first nationally representative survey of eating disorders in the U.S.—experts say physicians should routinely screen for binge eating disorder, especially among overweight and obese patients. Mental health clinicians, in particular, are in a good position to recognize and treat the disorder, and the issues of low self-esteem and poor body image that often accompany it.

Most physicians, however, aren't aware of the problem, says James [I.] Hudson, MD, director of the psychiatric epidemiology research program at McLean Hospital and a professor of psychiatry at Harvard.

"Doctors have a reasonable degree of awareness about anorexia and bulimia, but they're not tuned into binge eating. It's just not as well known," says Hudson, lead author of "The Prevalence and Correlates of Eating Disorders in the National Comorbidity Survey Replication." The study, published Feb. 1 [2007] in *Biological Psychiatry*, found that 2.8 percent of the general population has binge eating disorder—more than bulimia (1 percent prevalence) and anorexia (0.6 percent) combined. Findings reveal it's a "major public health problem."

The study also found that:

Binge eating disorder (BED) is strongly associated with severe obesity, which can lead to diabetes, heart disease, hypertension and stroke. Although eating disorders overall are about twice as common among women as men, 40 percent of binge eaters are men.

78.9 percent of those with binge eating disorder met the criteria for at least one other psychiatric disorder, and 48.9 percent met the criteria for three or more psychiatric disorders.

No single class of mental disorders stood out as being consistently associated with BED. Among those with binge eating disorder, 31.9 percent also met the criteria for social phobia, 32.3 percent for major depressive disorder, 26.3 percent for post-traumatic stress disorder, 23.3 percent for any substance use disorder, and 65.1 percent for any anxiety disorder.

62.6 percent of those with BED reported at least some role impairment at home, work and/or in their social life.

The average duration of BED was 8.1 years, compared with 8.3 for bulimia and 1.7 for anorexia. Less than half of those with binge eating disorder had sought treatment for it.

"Binge eating disorder represents a major public health problem," Hudson said. "It is imperative that health experts take notice of these findings."

While physicians are well aware of bulimia and anorexia, they tend to overlook binge eating, for reasons including its lack of obvious physical signs and its lack of official recognition. The American Psychiatric Association's *Diagnostic and Statistical Manual of Mental Disorders* (DSM-IV) currently classifies BED as an "eating disorder not otherwise specified" and needing further study. Many researchers, however, believe there is now sufficient evidence to classify it as a separate disorder. A working group for the next (fifth) edition of the DSM, to be published in 2012, is being formed to discuss and will decide the question.

Detection is also hampered by physicians' reluctance to raise the issue of eating disorders, Hudson notes. "It makes the doctor uncomfortable; it makes the patient uncomfortable. I don't like to ask about it myself. But we need to be asking about it."

Questions to Ask

Since binge eating is most common among the overweight and obese, those populations are the logical place to start screening. Binge eating is even more likely in overweight patients with low self-esteem and a poor body image.

Ruth Striegel-Moore, PhD—professor and chair of psychology at Wesleyan University and past president of the Academy for Eating Disorders—suggests starting the conversation with a simple question: "Do you feel you have any problems with your eating?"

If the patient says yes, the clinician should ask about these key signs of BED:

Do you eat unusually large amounts of food at one sitting (equivalent to two full meals)?

Do you eat this way even when you're not hungry?

Do you eat until you're uncomfortably full?

Do you feel you've lost control and can't stop eating?

Do you feel ashamed or depressed afterwards?

Has this happened two or more times a week for six months?

Do you eat alone because you're embarrassed to eat around others?

Not a Moral Flaw

It's important to ask these questions in a neutral way, being sensitive to the shame and stigma surrounding eating disorders, Hudson emphasizes. "They need to convey that this is not a moral flaw, but a medical problem to be addressed."

But Cynthia [M.] Bulik, PhD, director of the eating disorders program at the University of North Carolina [at Chapel Hill], has found that many patients want to talk about their binge eating, and are relieved when a healthcare provider asks about it. "I can't tell you the number of e-mails I've gotten from people on the street who have seen me discussing this. They say, 'Thank you so much for talking about it. I'm cutting this out and taking it to my doctor.'"

While there's sometimes a gray area between binge eating and simply overeating, the key distinguishing factors for BED are a loss of control when eating and feelings of distress after binges. Bingeing is often rooted in a patient's low self-esteem, poor body image, and the use of food to comfort oneself at times of stress.

Binge eating is also tied to all-or-nothing thinking, Bulik explains. "They think, well, I've already blown it by eating half this carton of ice cream; I might as well eat the rest of it."

Reassurance, Referral, Treatment Goals

If the patient indicates a problem with binge eating, the clinician should reassure him or her that it's a treatable condition and that help is available. The patient should also be evaluated for other mental disorders including anxiety and depression.

"The biggest mistake doctors make is to trivialize the problem and say, 'Well, we all overeat sometimes,' and to tell the patient to just control their eating. It's more complex than that," explains Striegel-Moore.

The treatment goals for BED are stopping the binges, losing weight, treating any comorbid disorders, and correcting the self-defeating feelings, thoughts and behaviors that lead to binges.

Where to Refer

To achieve these goals, many experts recommend a comprehensive eating disorders program. The programs take a multidisciplinary approach that typically includes nutrition coun-

How Frequently Do Binge Eating Disorder and Obesity Coexist?

The percentage of obese individuals who suffer from BED [binge eating disorder] varies greatly depending on the nature of the sample and the method used to diagnose BED. Several early studies using self-report methods found prevalences of BED as high as 20–30% in weight control samples as opposed to rates of 2–3% in mostly normal weight community samples. However, interview-based studies have reported significantly lower rates of BED in both types of samples, with rates as low as 1% in the general population and less than 5% in obesity treatment samples, although as many as 10–25% in weight loss samples report binge eating that does not meet formal criteria for BED. In epidemiological community samples, studies using both self-report and interview methods have consistently demonstrated an association between BED and weight, with rates of binge eating in overweight and obese subjects at least double those in normal weight individuals. Within the obese, it has long been known that rates of binge eating increase with increasing adiposity. Moreover, BED seems to be associated with early onset of obesity.

James E. Mitchell et al.
Binge-Eating Disorder: Clinical Foundations and Treatment.
New York: Guilford Press, 2008, pp. 25.

seling; a behavioral weight control plan with healthy meals spaced throughout the day; medication in some cases; and a strong foundation in cognitive behavioral therapy (CBT)— considered the gold standard for treating the disorder. According to an April 2006 evidence report on eating disorders, commissioned by the Agency for Healthcare Research and Quality [AHRQ], CBT is effective in reducing the number of binge days or the number of binge episodes, though it does not lead to significant weight loss.

Eating disorders programs are offered by most academic medical centers and many hospitals. Or patients can work with a therapist who specializes in CBT and eating disorders; the Academy for Eating Disorders and the Association for Behavioral and Cognitive Therapies offer online searches to find a therapist.

Because binge eating disorder is not an official diagnosis, insurance coverage is often minimal or nonexistent, and patients without coverage often can't afford to pay for treatments out of pocket—another reason some are urging official recognition for the disorder.

Self-Help a Viable Approach

For patients without coverage, and those wary of traditional therapy yet motivated to work on the problem, self-help treatment may be a viable option. The approach uses books or other materials to guide patients through a program built on cognitive behavioral therapy. Like traditional CBT, the programs help patients develop a structured eating plan and correct the self-defeating thoughts and behaviors that lead to binges.

"Say your in-laws are coming this weekend, and you know it's a stressor for you. You make a plan for how you're going to handle that without bingeing," says Striegel-Moore. According to studies in 1998 and 2001, self-help approaches were effective in reducing binges and improving patients' attitudes about eating. Recommended self-help books include *Overcoming Binge Eating* and *Getting Better Bit(e) by Bit(e)*.

And the newest frontier in self-help is computer-based programs. With a grant from the National Institute of Mental Health, for example, Bulik developed a program called Preventing Overweight with Exercise and Reasoning (POWER), which she describes as "therapy on a CD." The program uses realistic vignettes, self-paced lessons and interactive quizzes to help patients understand why they binge and to help them make better eating choices. "Patients love it because it's so interactive," Bulik says. "Computer-based programs are the future of self-help."

Other Approaches

While cognitive behavioral therapy is the most proven therapy for binge eating disorder, other approaches have shown promise, such as interpersonal therapy, which explores issues in the patient's relationships. A 2002 study which compared CBT with interpersonal therapy to treat 162 BED patients found recovery rates were equivalent in both groups.

And while some may believe a conventional diet program is the answer—from Atkins to Jenny Craig to Weight Watchers—the approach hasn't been well tested for treating binge eating disorder. Some studies have found that BED patients lose as much weight as non-BED patients in traditional weight-control programs. But some experts advise against the approach.

"My experience is, by the time patients are talking to their doctor about this problem they've already tried dieting programs and it didn't help," Hudson says. Furthermore, "some of these programs say, 'Our program can't fail—it's you who failed.' So if the patient doesn't succeed, they feel worse than before."

The Role of Medications

Although there is no FDA [Food and Drug Administration]-approved drug specifically for binge eating disorder, several medications have been found effective in clinical trials.

- Selective serotonin reuptake inhibitors (SSRIs) are most commonly used to treat BED. In randomized trials, they have been found more effective at reducing binge eating than in inducing weight loss.

- Some appetite suppressants have been shown to reduce binge eating and body weight in patients with BED.

- A small number of anticonvulsant medications have been tested in clinical trials for BED, and have been shown to decrease binges and reduce weight. The drugs often have troublesome side effects, however, including dizziness, fatigue and difficulty concentrating.

The question of whether and when to use medication ultimately depends on the patient's, and the doctor's, preference. Hudson recommends first trying CBT, and if the patient doesn't show sufficient improvement, medication can be tried, either alone or with therapy. Striegel-Moore recommends using medication primarily for patients with comorbid anxiety or depression, and using it to complement, not replace, therapy. The AHRQ evidence report states that "combining medication and CBT may improve both binge eating and weight loss, although sufficient trials have not been done to determine which medications are best at producing weight loss."

No Magic Bullet

Unfortunately, successful treatment for binge eating disorder is neither quick nor easy, and relapses are common. Even the most effective treatments take 10–12 weeks to work. And, for reasons that aren't fully understood, the treatments that have helped patients stop bingeing have shown little success in helping them lose weight. This underscores the need for further study and better treatments—and the importance of perseverance for those struggling to overcome binge eating. "It's incredibly hard to lose weight long term," Striegel-Moore says.

"We live stressful lives, we're surrounded by cheap unhealthy food, and we don't exercise enough. For anyone to get control over binge eating requires truly lasting behavioral change."

"*It is our attitude about obesity that may put us at greatest risk.*"

The Obesity Epidemic Is a Myth That Promotes Unhealthy Weight Loss

Linda Bacon

Linda Bacon is a nutrition professor in the biology department at City College of San Francisco and associate nutritionist at the University of California, Davis. In the following viewpoint, excerpted from her book Health at Every Size: The Surprising Truth About Your Weight, *Bacon argues that the obesity epidemic is a myth promoting unhealthy ideas about weight. According to Bacon, this includes misperceptions that obesity is deadly, weight loss improves health, and weight can be controlled. Bacon also maintains that heavier people are more likely to try harmful dieting methods, experience dangerous cycles of weight loss and gain, and suffer from size-based discrimination.*

As you read, consider the following questions:

1. What is the recalculated number of deaths related to obesity each year, as provided by Bacon?

2. What example does Bacon offer of dangerous weight-loss methods used to treat obesity?

3. How does the author back her statement that feeling fat has stronger health effects than being fat?

More than 400,000 Americans die of overweight and obesity every year, so many that it may soon surpass smoking as the leading cause of preventable death. At least that's what the Centers for Disease Control [and Prevention] (CDC) told us in the prestigious *Journal of the American Medical Association (JAMA)*. Their report grabbed headlines, helped along by dramatic, well-distributed press releases from the CDC and *JAMA*, and resulted in tens of thousands of citations in the popular press and thousands more in scientific journals.

But an updated federal report acknowledged that the analysis suffered from computational errors. Using better methodology and newer data, CDC epidemiologists *reduced the estimate fifteen-fold*, determining that obesity and overweight are only associated with an excess of 26,000 annual deaths, far fewer than guns, alcohol, or car crashes.

Separating overweight from obesity reveals further interesting information. First, *"overweight" people live longer than "normal" weight people.* (There were 86,000 fewer deaths a year in the overweight category than in the normal range.) Next, the excess deaths in the obesity category were clustered in the more extreme range (body mass index [BMI] greater than 35), which is not where the majority of obese Americans fall (BMI 30 to 35).

Most striking is that the CDC did not publicize the new results, nor change their public health message. After all, they used the original study to justify their war on obesity. Why not stop the war now that the evidence has disappeared? And if they are so concerned about the health of "overweight" people, why isn't this news cause for celebration?

Basic Truisms?

The CDC didn't just overhype a crisis, they helped invent it. With only 26,000 victims, we don't have an obesity (and overweight) epidemic; our epidemic is one of fearmongering and ignorance. Consider the following statements:

1. Overweight and obesity lead to early death.

2. Overweight and obesity lead to disease.

3. We are gaining weight at epidemic rates.

4. Weight loss improves health and longevity.

5. You control what you weigh.

6. Anyone can keep lost weight off if she or he tries hard enough.

7. Thinner is more attractive.

8. We can trust the experts to provide accurate information.

For most of us, these statements seem like basic truisms. However, much of what we believe to be true about weight—*including all of the statements above*—is in fact myth, fueled by the power of money and cultural bias. Public health officials, health advocates, and scientists are complicit (often unintentionally) in supporting and encouraging the lies. The campaign against obesity is not about science or health; its misconceptions about the most basic research are astounding. If you suspend your preconceptions and open yourself to the scientific evidence, a very different picture emerges.

The "Death by Fat" Myth

No obesity myth is more potent than the one that says obesity kills. It gives us permission to call our fear of fat a health concern, rather than naming it as the cultural oppression it is.

That "obesity kills" has been the backbone of the federal public health campaign. Yet, "it is still far from certain whether there is any measurable mortality toll at all among overweight and obese Americans as a group," writes Centers for Disease Control [and Prevention] epidemiologist Katherine Flegal and colleagues in *JAMA*. Their research found that "even severe obesity failed to show up as a statistically significant mortality risk" and suggested that overweight may actually be protective.

This finding is not new news, but entirely consistent with the bulk of the literature. All these well-respected studies cited below, for instance, determined that overweight people were living at least as long as, and frequently longer than, normal weight people:

- The Established Populations for the Epidemiologic Studies of the Elderly investigation (included more than 8,000 senior citizens)

- The Study of Osteoporotic Fractures investigation (included more than 8,000 women)

- The Cardiovascular Health Study (included almost 5,000 individuals)

- Women's Health Initiative Observational Study (included 90,000 women)

- An investigation of almost 170,000 adults in China

- An investigation of 20,000 German construction workers

- An investigation of 12,000 Finnish women

- An investigation of 1.7 million Norwegians (Yes, you read that right: 1.7 million people! In this, the largest epidemiological study ever conducted, the highest life expectancy is among individuals who are overweight by our current standards and the lowest life expectancy is among those defined as underweight. What's more, individuals who fit into what is deemed the ideal weight range had a lower life expectancy than some of those who were obese.)

These are not a few errant investigations, but representative of conclusions that dominate the research. The most comprehensive review, for instance, pooled data from twenty-six studies and concluded that overweight individuals were living slightly longer than those of normal weight.

The scientific evidence is clear: *Body fat is not the killer it's portrayed as.*

The "Disease-Promoting Fat" Myth

The idea that weight plays a large causal role in disease is also unproven. Little evidence supports that weight is the primary cause of many diseases for which it is routinely blamed, except osteoarthritis, sleep apnea, and possibly a few cancers. In contrast, there are several diseases for which high levels of body fat provide a distinct, though rarely acknowledged, advantage.

It is clear that weight is *associated* with increased risk for some diseases, but causation is an entirely different matter. In some cases, the causality may travel in the opposite direction, as in the case of diabetes. . . . Some of the medications intended to treat weight-associated diseases may also encourage weight gain, such as the insulin, sulfonylureas, and thiazolidinediones used to treat diabetes.

Lifestyle habits can also confuse the picture. A sedentary lifestyle, for example, may predispose someone to weight gain *and* make them more vulnerable to many diseases. It is well established that the relationship between activity and longevity is stronger than the relationship between weight and longevity. Consider the research conducted as part of the Aerobics Center Longitudinal Study in Texas, which found that obese men who are classified as "fit" based on a treadmill test have death rates just as low as "fit" lean men. Moreover, the fit obese men had death rates one-half those of the lean but unfit men, indicating that fitness is more important than weight in longevity. Similar results were demonstrated for women.

Damaging Cycles

Larger people may be more likely to have tried dangerous weight-loss methods, which may also be reflected in higher incidence of disease. For instance, in 1970, 8 percent of all U.S. prescriptions were for amphetamines intended to treat obesity that are now known to increase heart disease risk. Heavier people may also have gone through damaging cycles of losing and regaining weight, making them more prone to certain diseases. For instance, even a single cycle of losing and regaining weight may damage blood vessels and increase risk for cardiovascular disease.

Reduced access to health care and reluctance to seek health care for fear of discrimination may also confuse the picture. And of course, stress from the discrimination and widespread hostility directed at larger people may also be a significant contributor to the risks currently blamed on body fat alone. Researchers find larger people experience more cynical mistrust, which is highly associated with inflammation, a major risk for heart disease.

It is well established that obesity is higher among ethnic minorities and people of lower socioeconomic status, both of which are also highly associated with disease risk. The higher pollution levels in poorer neighborhoods may play a role, and the increased discrimination to which ethnic minorities and people of lower socioeconomic status are subject may be a factor as well.

The Prevalence of Weight Discrimination

I suspect that it is our attitude about obesity that may put us at greatest risk. Cross-cultural studies suggest that larger people are not subject to the same diseases in countries where there are fewer stigmas attached to weight. Also, in the United States, there is a stronger relationship between BMI and morbidity (disease) and mortality (early death) among groups more negatively affected by body image concerns (younger people, Caucasians, and women). Even more telling, when researchers looked at a nationally representative group of more than 170,000 U.S. adults, they found the difference between actual weight and perceived ideal weight was a better indicator of mental and physical health than BMI. In other words, *feeling* fat has stronger health effects than *being* fat.

This finding is not surprising. It is well established that stigma produces stress, which in turn is a risk factor for many diseases, including diabetes and cardiovascular disease. And of course, weight discrimination is pervasive and severe. In fact, the prevalence of weight discrimination has even surpassed discrimination based on race and gender.

Periodical and Internet Sources Bibliography

The following articles have been selected to supplement the diverse views presented in this chapter.

Jessica Bennett	"It's Not Just White Girls," *Newsweek*, September 5, 2008.
Frank Bruni	"I Was a Baby Bulimic," *New York Times Magazine*, July 15, 2009.
Kathy Chu	"Extreme Dieting Spreads in Asia," *USA Today*, March 29, 2010.
Randi Hutter Epstein	"When Eating Disorders Strike in Midlife," *New York Times*, July 13, 2009.
Corinna Hübener	"Eating Disorders: A Modern Epidemic," *Grail World*, January/February/March 2009.
Nalea J. Ko	"Asian Americans Weigh In on Body Image Issues," *Pacific Citizen*, March 4, 2011.
Shelley Levitt	"The Disordered Eating Epidemic," *More*, October 2010.
Kathleen McGuire	"Food Obsessed? The Dangerous Line Between Order and Disorder," *Dance Magazine*, October 2010.
Robin Nixon	"Grown Up but Eat Like a Kid? You May Have 'Selective Eating Disorder,'" msnbc.com, November 28, 2010. www.msnbc.msn.com.
Elizabeth Palmberg	"Body Language," *Sojourners*, April 2009.
Emily Yoffe	"Stuffed! How to Stop Binge Eating," *O, The Oprah Magazine*, August 2007.

OPPOSING
VIEWPOINTS®
SERIES

CHAPTER 2

What Causes Eating Disorders?

Chapter Preface

In the development of anorexia or bulimia in children, parents with eating disorders are often considered a factor. "Eating rituals, obsessive preoccupations with food and body image concerns are central to the eating disordered mind, distracting parents from their need to focus on the child's needs," states psychotherapist Abigail H. Natenshon on the EmpoweredParents website. "Children are not born healthy eaters. They learn from parents how to eat, how to feel about what they eat, and how to care for their body." While Natenshon does not believe parents can be a direct cause, she maintains that "parental beliefs, attitudes and examples set can do a great deal to shape a child's attitudes, and may contribute to triggering a child's genetic susceptibility to developing disease."

Others suggest eating disorders can be a reaction to conflict with parents or stress within the family. "Here, kids will cling to whatever they can to get by—and yes, in these cases, cutting, drinking, binging, and sometimes starving are all symptoms used to cope," suggests Judith Brisman, director of the Eating Disorder Resource Center, in the *Huffington Post*. "Thus, in some families, there is such stress that many symptoms develop in the kids—eating disorders among them—as means of dealing with intolerable feelings."

On the other hand, Brisman claims that anorexia and bulimia both have a genetic basis, and society's idealization of thinness can override the influences of parents or families on children, whether their relationships are healthy or not. "In our demanding and bodily obsessed culture . . . this gene lights up like wildfire, and serious eating disorders can be set into play. This has nothing to do with family dynamics and can erupt in any family environment," Brisman maintains.

In the following chapter, the authors deliberate the origins and causes of eating disorders.

"*Some people are born more vulnerable than others to developing an eating disorder. . . .*"

Genetics Play a Significant Role in Eating Disorders

Johanna S. Kandel

Johanna S. Kandel is the founder and executive director of the Alliance for Eating Disorders Awareness and author of Life Beyond Your Eating Disorder: Reclaim Yourself, Regain Your Health, Recover for Good. *In the following viewpoint, excerpted from* Life Beyond Your Eating Disorder, *she claims that clinical studies have determined that eating disorders have a strong genetic component. Additionally, researchers have linked the disruption of serotonin levels in the brain to appetite, Kandel states, thus influencing food restriction or bingeing. She continues that environmental influences—which often idealize thinness—and lifestyle choices can increase the risk of genetically predisposed eating disorders.*

As you read, consider the following questions:

1. How does Thomas R. Insel describe anorexia nervosa?

2. What is Kandel's opinion of dealing with images and messages that associate thinness with perfection?

3. How should information supporting the genetic basis of eating disorders be used by people with anorexia or bulimia?

One of the most exciting and enlightening moments of my life came when I learned that research indicates there is a genetic component to eating disorders. Some people are born more vulnerable than others to developing an eating disorder, and various researchers have linked the problem to the disruption of serotonin levels in the brain. Serotonin is a neurotransmitter, a brain chemical whose functions include the regulation of both mood and appetite. Some researchers have theorized that increased serotonin levels may leave people in a perpetual state of anxiety, leading them to gain some sense of control by restricting food intake. Low serotonin levels, on the other hand, could lead to bingeing on foods high in carbohydrates, which would temporarily raise serotonin levels and elevate mood.

A Brain Disease

In a strange way it was extremely liberating for me to read the following statement made by Dr. Thomas R. Insel, director of the National Institute of Mental Health, in an October 5, 2006, letter to the chief executive officer of the National Eating Disorders Association:

> Research tells us that anorexia nervosa is a brain disease with severe metabolic effects on the entire body. While the symptoms are behavioral, this illness has a biological core, with genetic components, changes in brain activity, and neural pathways currently under study.

While you might think it would be disturbing for me to learn that anorexia was a brain disease, it was actually validating to know that there was a biological explanation for my problem. And Dr. Insel didn't leave me feeling powerless, because he went on to say that "most women with anorexia recover, usually following intensive psychological and medical care." So, it is truly not your fault that you have an eating disorder. Even better, it *is* possible to recover—and you shouldn't be expected to cure it all on your own.

Simply telling someone with an eating disorder to "just get over it and sit down and eat" is never going to work. What are you supposed to say to that? "Oh yeah, you're right. For all those years I was struggling with anorexia the real problem was that I just forgot to eat, but now that you've reminded me I'll remember. Thanks!" No! Initially, I'd actually thought it *would* be that easy. I thought I could just sit down, eat a meal and not restrict, binge or act out. But, of course, it wasn't easy. It isn't, and it's not supposed to be. But now I have a valid, scientific explanation not only for why I'd developed an eating disorder but also for why recovery wasn't so easy.

Walter [H.] Kaye, MD, of the University of Pittsburgh Medical Center, working with an international group of doctors, has collected information from more than six hundred families in which two or more members had an eating disorder. In an article titled "Genetics Research: Why Is It Important to the Field of Eating Disorders?" Craig Johnson, PhD, director of the Eating Disorders Program at Laureate Psychiatric Clinic and Hospital in Tulsa, Oklahoma, states that these results may be nothing short of a breakthrough. They suggest that both anorexia and bulimia "are as heritable as other psychiatric illnesses such as schizophrenia, depression, anxiety and obsessive-compulsive disorders." And other clinical studies have also supported this evidence. One, conducted at the University of North Carolina at Chapel Hill, reviewed information from more than thirty-one thousand people in the Swedish Twin Registry and determined that genetics is responsible for 56 percent of a person's risk of developing an eating disorder—with environmental factors determining the rest.

Our Environment and Lifestyle Choices

As with almost all diseases and conditions, genetics may predispose us to being more susceptible, but our environment and lifestyle choices either increase or decrease our chances of actually getting the disease. According to Dr. Kaye, "We think genes load the gun by creating behavioral susceptibility, such as perfectionism or the drive for thinness. Environment then pulls the trigger." The problem, of course, is that if we know, for example, that we're predisposed to developing high blood pressure, we can avoid eating salty foods. But we can't remove ourselves from the world, and the world we live in is filled with messages and images that hold up thinness as a measure of perfection. All we can do is try to nurture our children's self-esteem and help them to develop a healthy body image.

As I thought about Dr. Kaye's words, I realized that when I started down my path to anorexia and bulimia, all I wanted to do was better myself, and I was in an environment that encouraged me to lose weight and be thin. I truly believed that if I lost weight I'd be a better dancer, and that was the most important thing in my life, the only thing I really cared about. So, not only my own perfectionism but also the environment in which I'd immersed myself were working together to put me at risk for developing an eating disorder.

In the Family

When I ask members of my support groups whether there's anyone else in their family with an eating disorder, I see a lot of people shaking their heads no. And then I ask, "Well, what about your aunt Suzy or uncle Bob, who will only eat particular foods, has peculiar eating habits or is exercising all the time?" and all of a sudden their eyes light up and hands go into the air.

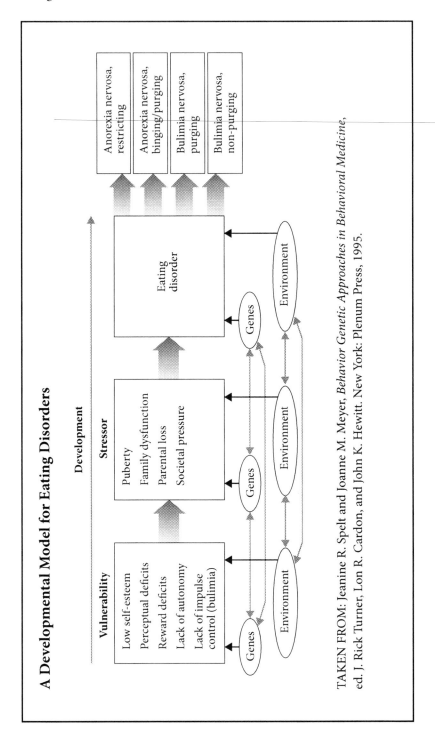

A Developmental Model for Eating Disorders

Development

Vulnerability	Stressor
Low self-esteem	Puberty
Perceptual deficits	Family dysfunction
Reward deficits	Parental loss
Lack of autonomy	Societal pressure
Lack of impulse control (bulimia)	

Eating disorder

Genes

Environment

Anorexia nervosa, restricting

Anorexia nervosa, binging/purging

Bulimia nervosa, purging

Bulimia nervosa, non-purging

TAKEN FROM: Jeanine R. Spelt and Joanne M. Meyer, *Behavior Genetic Approaches in Behavioral Medicine*, ed. J. Rick Turner, Lon R. Cardon, and John K. Hewitt. New York: Plenum Press, 1995.

Looking back on it now, I can see that not only eating disorders but also alcoholism, depression and anxiety run in my family. I remember being a little girl and visiting an aunt, my father's sister, who worked for a large clothing store in Paris. She was petite and thin, and I recall her telling me that her secret to being skinny was to eat just one fast-food fish fillet sandwich a day. At the time, I didn't think, *Okay, I'm going to do that*, but it did reinforce the idea that weight was an issue and that thinness was something to work for. And now, of course, I know that my aunt must have had some kind of eating disorder—or disordered eating—herself.

In addition to what I observed in my father's family, my mother's sisters have also struggled with poor body image and have always been extremely conscious of everything they ate. So, in fact, there were eating and body image issues on both sides of my family. For me, the genetic gun was definitely loaded and just waiting for the environmental circumstances that would pull the trigger. I really didn't roll out of bed one morning and decide to be anorexic!

"The modality of interaction between
genetic and environmental factors, and
the extent to which genetic factors are
involved in the susceptibility to eating
disorders, are unresolved issues."

Genetics May Not
Play a Significant Role
in Eating Disorders

Simona Giordano

*Simona Giordano is Reader of Bioethics at the School of Law at
the University of Manchester in England. In the following viewpoint, excerpted from her book* Exercise and Eating Disorders:
An Ethical and Legal Analysis, *Giordano writes that the role of
genetics in eating disorders is unclear. While the rates of the diseases are higher among identical twins than fraternal twins, she
states, this does not necessarily mean that genes cause eating disorders—studies on separated twins would give more precise information but such studies do not exist. Giordano adds that genetics cannot explain several aspects of eating disorders, and
despite family history, non-shared environmental experiences of
each individual can play an important factor.*

Simona Giordano, *Exercise and Eating Disorders: An Ethical and Legal Analysis.* Andover,
Hampshire: Routledge, 2010. Reproduced by permission of the publisher.

As you read, consider the following questions:

1. What are two types of multifactorial diseases, as explained by Giordano?

2. Why is the interpretation of incidence of family not straightforward in studies of eating disorders, as explained by Giordano?

3. In Giordano's view, why is the relationship of changing opioid and dopamine levels and eating disorders unclear?

Eating disorders are thought to result from a complex interplay between environmental and genetic risk factors. When a disorder results from many different causes, in scientific language it is said that *its etiology is heterogeneous*. Diseases with heterogeneous etiology are known as *complex or multifactorial diseases*. It seems that eating disorders must be explained in a multifactorial manner.

There are two types of multifactorial diseases: in one type, only a small number of genes behave differently from normality (gene variants). In these cases the genetic component is said to be *oligogenic*. In the other type, there are many gene variants that act simultaneously and interact: here the genetic component is said to be *polygenic*.

It is unclear whether eating disorders might have an oligogenic or polygenic genetic component, because, as we are going to see, studies on the genetics of eating disorders have not yet provided conclusive answers.

Many healthy people in the general population may present the genetic variants that contribute to complex diseases (both oligogenic and polygenic), but do not develop the diseases for which they carry the genes. This means that these gene variants are not necessarily deleterious and it is not certain that they *will cause* the disease.

So, what causes *some* individuals to develop certain multi-factorial diseases, if the gene variants alone are not sufficient to cause them?

Genes and Environment: A Mysterious Interplay

Despite the fact that genetic abnormalities are not solely responsible for eating disorders, many scientists seem to agree that genetic predisposition plays an important role in the development of eating disorders. Yet the modality of interaction between genetic and environmental factors, and the extent to which genetic factors are involved in susceptibility to eating disorders, are unresolved issues. It is likely that the interplay between genetics, environmental influences, and the individual's interpretation of these factors in one person's articulation of behavior is very difficult, if not impossible, to capture.

Anorexia and bulimia nervosa are found to be "statistically more common among family members" than in the general population. Studies on twins have shown a concomitance of 50 percent between monozygotic (or identical) twins, as compared with 10 percent of dizygotic twins.

This concordance is called the 'concordance rate'. Dizygotic twins are those twins who have different DNA; they are not identical, but happen to share the womb at the same time. The greater concordance rates among monozygotic twins as compared to the concordance rates among dizygotic twins is generally taken as evidence of a "strong etiological role for genetic factors".

In other words, among identical twins, it is quite likely that if one has an eating disorder, the other has it too. Among non-identical twins, even if they are also raised in the same environment and born at the same time, it is five times less likely that both of them will develop an eating disorder. This seems to indicate that, since identical twins have the same DNA and non-identical twins do not, genetics is some-how responsible for eating disorders.

However, the greater concordance among identical twins does not necessarily mean that genetics is the cause of eating disorders. To render these results more reliable, it would be necessary to study identical twins brought up separately, and to assess whether there is also a concordance rate among iden-tical twins brought up separately, and what this is. Studying separated twins would give us more precise information on the effective influence of genetics on individuals' behavior and predisposition to diseases. However, to date, there have been no adoption studies of eating disorders among separated monozygotic twins.

There are also methodological difficulties with case ascer-tainment, and scientists recognize the low statistical power of available studies.

The interpretation of familiality (incidence within a family) is thus not straightforward. Some studies "strongly suggest that the familiality observed in family studies is pri-marily due to genetic causes"; other studies suggest that this familiality is likely to result from both environmental and ge-netic influences. Some researchers argue that genetics is the most determining factor—or that there is a genetic predispo-sition to anorexia, which becomes manifest due to environ-mental stressors, such as inappropriate diet or emotional dis-tress; other researchers stress the importance of environmental stressors—and argue that environmental influences play a ma-jor role in determining the onset of eating disorders.

Non-Shared Environmental Experiences

Some researchers have noticed that genetic explanations can-not capture a number of aspects of eating disorders. They ar-gue that *non-shared environmental experiences* are also signifi-cant in the genesis of the disorder. Non-shared environmental experiences are those unique to each individual, despite the fact that they live in the same family. For example, two siblings may share the same genetic makeup, the same family and the same environment, but while some experiences will be similar, other experiences and influences will be *non-shared*, that is, unique to each individual. Monozygotic and dizygotic twin studies can thus also be used to understand the importance of non-shared environmental experiences in the development of eating disorders.

In short, genes might be involved in the onset of eating disorders. However, genes do not seem to be solely responsible for these conditions. In other conditions, genes are to a very large extent, or completely, responsible for the symptoms. Tay-Sachs disease, for example, is a neurodegenerative disorder entirely caused by mutations in the HEXA gene. Muscular dystrophy is another example of a genetic disorder where the environmental stressors might play a role in retarding or containing the degeneration, but which is largely determined by genetic mutations. The case of eating disorders is different from primarily genetic disorders. In eating disorders, genetics, in interplay with environmental factors, individual sensitivity and social pressure, contributes, in a somehow mysterious way, to generate these still scarcely understood conditions.

Other researchers, rather than focusing on the genes, have suggested that eating disorders are caused by dysfunctions in the central nervous system. It is to this suggestion that I now move.

The Brain: The Central Nervous System

There seems to be evidence that people with eating disorders have altered brain structures. In some cases, the alteration is still present after the disorder in eating is corrected. In view of these alterations and of the symptoms of eating disorders, some experts have suggested that anorexia and bulimia nervosa may be caused by a disorder in the neurotransmitter system. Neurotransmitters are elements present in our central nervous system, which are responsible for the transmission of signals within the brain. Some of these neurotransmitters seem altered in eating-disordered patients.

In particular, dopamine is responsible for giving us the sense of hunger and satiety, and therefore some scientists think that it may be involved in eating disorders. Endorphins and serotonin are generally associated with states of well-being and excitement. In eating-disordered people, the levels of these neurotransmitters are unbalanced.

It has also been suggested that opioids may play a role in generating eating disorders. Opioids influence eating: they increase the desire to eat, whereas opioid antagonists decrease it. Several researchers have noticed that the level of opioids in both anorexics and bulimics is higher than normal.

The relationship between the change in the rate of opioids, dopamine and eating disorders is, however, unclear. Although there is an association between eating disorders and imbalances in the neurotransmitter system, many of these imbalances seem to be the consequence of eating disorders, and tend to return to normal levels as weight is gained. Abnormalities in the level of serotonin may in some cases persist after weight gain and it has therefore been hypothesized that a disorder in serotonin may create a vulnerability to anorexia and bulimia. The causality, however, has not been established.

The central nervous system thus remains a fertile field of investigation for research into the causes of eating disorders, but research is still ongoing.

> "Media images establish what it means
> to be a beautiful woman in our soci-
> ety."

Cultural Obsession with Thinness Is Harmful

Michelle M. Lelwica

Michelle M. Lelwica is a religion professor at Concordia College and author of The Religion of Thinness: Satisfying the Spiritual Hungers Behind Women's Obsession with Food and Weight. *In the following viewpoint, excerpted from* The Religion of Thinness, *Lelwica declares that thinness is worshipped in American culture. Unrealistic body images are promoted in the media and entertainment, she insists, resulting in greater numbers of women and men who feel "too fat" and suffer from eating disorders. Lelwica compares this obsession with eating and weight to a "religion of thinness," wherein dieting offers control, belonging, and the hope that health and happiness can be attained through the "perfect" body.*

As you read, consider the following questions:

1. How much do Americans spend each year trying to lose weight, as stated by Lelwica?

Michelle M. Lelwica, *The Religion of Thinness: Satisfying the Spiritual Hungers Behind Women's Obsession with Food and Weight*. Carlsbad, CA: Gürze, 2009. © 2009 by Michelle M. Lelwica. All rights reserved. Reproduced by permission of Gürze Books, LLC.

2. How does the author describe the type of women who appear on magazine covers?

3. What rituals does the religion of thinness provide, as claimed by Lelwica?

We live in a culture that worships thinness.

Americans spend over $60 billion per year trying to shed their "excess" flesh. Sales for weight loss products—from appetite suppressants to home-delivered diet foods—are steadily on the rise. We are constantly bombarded with TV commercials and infomercials, Internet spam and banners, radio and print media advertisements—all peddling ways to help us tighten and trim. Marketing gurus in the book publishing industry refer to January as "New Year New You"—walk into any bookstore franchise during this critical sales season and you'll find it stacked with titles designed to help you lose weight, look "great," and live "right." Perhaps not surprisingly, diet books outsell any other books on the market—except the Bible.

The weight loss industry is, however, only part of the picture.

The Paradigm of Female Beauty

Need to buy groceries? You can't miss the "women's magazines" at the checkout counter. The cover of almost every one depicts a celebrity or model that both defines and is defined by a very narrow and relatively precise paradigm of female beauty. She is tall (maybe 5'10"), slender (about 110 pounds), and her body is meticulously toned. She is often a Barbie-type: white, blue-eyed, and blond-haired, although this long-standing tradition is shifting to include more women of color. Alongside these "beautiful" (skinny) women are the familiar headlines: "Lose 10 Pounds in 10 Days," "Fight Flab! Look Fab!"—or some variation on this monotonous theme. And, if you get bored staring at the collage of fat-free beauties while you're waiting to pay for your groceries, you can always look at the *un*flattering pictures of these same women in tabloids with accusatory headlines about their extreme weight gain or loss.

Media images establish what it means to be a beautiful woman in our society. It doesn't matter that the vast majority of us don't look like the women we are taught to adore. In fact, that's part of the ploy: The relative rarity of the "ideal" creates tremendous pressure for ordinary women to "improve" their appearance. Weight loss is essential to this transformation, or so we are told with both words and pictures. And the more we come to believe this truth, the more we absorb other messages as well—ones that are less obvious (and perhaps more insidious for being so), but no less powerful. These messages teach us that our souls will only feel as good as our bodies look; that we can never be happy unless we strive for physical perfection; and that to be successful, loved, and satisfied we must try to emulate the images we have come to idolize.

"Too Fat"

Little wonder that in this cultural milieu the numbers of women with eating and body image problems are skyrocketing among female undergraduates. Some studies have shown that up to 20 percent of college women suffer from an eating disorder. Another found that 40 percent of college women showed "anorexic-like" behavior—nearly half of them engaged in bingeing and purging—and all of them knew someone else with similarly disordered behaviors. Another study discovered that a third of college women surveyed reported using "diet aids" in the past twelve months, including diet pills, fat blockers, diuretics, and laxatives. There have even been reports of plumbing problems in dormitories due to widespread vomiting. Binge eating without purging is more common than anorexia and bulimia combined. One survey found that 67 percent of college women binge eat.

These behaviors are extremely debilitating—if not deadly. Anorexia nervosa has the highest mortality rate of any psychiatric illness, and survivors often spend months in the hospital and years in treatment. However, anorexia, bulimia, and binge eating are only one part of a broad continuum of difficulties women have with food, weight and body image.

How many times have you tried to lose weight? How many hours have you spent preoccupied with the size of your waist, hips, or thighs?

If your answer is "too many," you are hardly alone. More than three-quarters of healthy-weight adult women in the U.S. believe they are "too fat," and nearly two-thirds of high school girls are on diets. Attempts to lose weight start very young: Eighty percent of fourth-grade girls surveyed said they had already been on diets. The same percentage of women in their mid-50s express a desire to be thinner. Meanwhile, growing numbers of women of color are joining the ranks of those who chronically hate their bodies, and more and more men are worrying about the "spare tire" around their midriffs or the layer of flesh that sags from their chins.

Many people spend a lifetime struggling with their weight. Why? Is it really to fend off the health-related dangers we hear so much about and have come to fear? To be sure, the physical ailments that some studies link to excess weight—heart disease, diabetes, and certain types of cancer—are well known and cause for alarm. Indeed, many of us are more prone to eat too much and exercise too little than to over-abstain or exercise excessively. But, weight loss is a precarious strategy for "getting fit," especially in light of the growing evidence suggesting that thinner is not *necessarily* healthier. Some studies raise questions about whether being moderately overweight is automatically unhealthy and whether it should be treated at all. In fact, research verifies that, like happiness and beauty,

Normalizing the Abnormal

Most women have learned to dislike their bodies, and many have also learned to distrust their appetites. In an advertisement for a Jell-O sugar-free pudding, . . . , the text reads, "Dessert? It's always on the tip of my tongue. Really, I mean, if I'm not eating dessert, I'm talking about it. If I'm not talking about it, I'm eating it. And I'm always thinking about it. . . ." What the advertisement is doing is normalizing something that is abnormal. The woman in the advertisement is preoccupied with food and this is a symptom of starvation. The advertisement seems to suggest that being in a starvation state is something that is to be expected, and to be dealt with by eating copious amounts of diet foods.

Karin Jasper, "Messages from the Media,"
National Eating Disorder Information Centre, 1994.
www.nedic.ca.

health is possible in a wide variety of shapes and sizes. In the end, health risks may have less to do with our drive for thinness than other, less tangible factors.

The Religion of Thinness

I propose that our obsessions with eating and weight mask the deeper needs of our spirits. We are looking for a way to maintain peace, order, and security in a world that seems out of control. We want to be happy and healthy, to feel accepted and connected within a larger community. We need to sense that our lives are meaningful, that we have a greater purpose.

The traditional way to manage these kinds of spiritual yearnings has been through religion. In the West, Christianity has been the predominant faith since the 4th century. However, in today's world the authority of Christianity, as well as other organized religions, is contested and in some ways declining. This has made it possible for women in our culture to break out of the constraining roles they had been kept in for so long, but it has also created a vacuum, a feeling that something is missing. The need for meaningful symbols, beliefs, stories, and rituals by which to organize our lives and understand our purpose has not disappeared. In fact, we are starving for them.

In an attempt to fill this void, many women have adopted what I call "The Religion of Thinness." This "religion" teaches us that controlling our weight will give us a feeling of control over our lives. It offers us the hope of health and happiness through the idea of the "perfect" body, which we believe is attainable through diet and exercise. It teaches us to feel morally superior if we "eat right" (meaning fewer fat grams or calories), and connects us to a larger community of women who are trying to lose weight. It gives us rituals—like counting and burning calories—that create a sense of order. And it includes a plethora of icons and symbols in the form of models and actresses in whose image we are encouraged to re-create ourselves. Perhaps most importantly of all, it gives us an ultimate purpose—the "salvation" that comes from being thin.

But in the end, its promises are hollow. The Religion of Thinness cannot fill the emptiness we feel inside ourselves. It cannot satisfy our deepest hungers. The hope it offers is an illusion, one that we have been fed by the media and other sources, and one that many of us have consumed with a religious-like fervor in our quest for meaning and purpose.

I know, because I too was once a disciple.

| "We need to celebrate women of all shapes and sizes, from petite to plus-size."

Some Perceptions of Thinness Are Unfair and Harmful

Julia Cheng

In the following viewpoint, Julia Cheng contends that thin women are scrutinized and unfairly judged. As an extremely slender person, Cheng recounts experiences in which others negatively commented on her weight or lack of curves, including allegations of self-starvation, and pressured her to eat. She applauds the "real beauty" movement that celebrates average and plus-size women, but objects that normally thin women are excluded and left to defend their body types. Cheng is a community associate at East-West School of International Studies in Flushing, New York.

As you read, consider the following questions:

1. What do people say about extremely slender women, as told by Cheng?

2. According to Cheng, what happens when she talks about her body image problems?

Julia Cheng, "In Defense of Skinny Girls," AliveMagazine.org, July 6, 2009. Reproduced by permission of the author.

3. What is Cheng's opinion of how the media portrays women's bodies?

"You know, you're freakishly skinny." "Don't you eat anything?"

"Real women have curves." "Guys like girls with some meat on them, not a bag of bones."

I'm 5 feet 4 inches tall, and I weigh 93 pounds. My wrist measures about 4 inches around.

I have always been incredibly thin, but I assumed that I would "fill out" as I grew older. I'm 22 now, and not much has changed. For most of my life I have hated my body.

I have trouble putting on weight, the same way some people struggle to lose weight. My only health problem, ironically enough, is extremely high cholesterol, which I inherited from my parents. During my freshman year of college, I managed to put on 15 pounds by loading up on pizza and ice cream at the cafeteria every day. Everyone told me how healthy and great I looked. I couldn't run for 5 minutes without wheezing and I struggled with irritable bowel syndrome. That was the only time in my life I was at a "healthy" weight. It's not possible for me unless I make myself sick.

"You Don't Understand How Lucky You Are"

"You don't understand how lucky you are. So many girls would kill to be skinny and have your 'problem.'"

If it was so great to be skinny, then why did I feel terrible about myself? And why did people go out of their way to attack my body on a daily basis?

New friends, old friends, and coworkers question my self-esteem, mental stability, and professional competence because they suspect I must be intentionally hurting myself to look the way I do. At family dinners, food is shoved onto my plate and my parents are shamed for not taking care of me. Strangers on the bus whisper about how sad it is that girls feel like they have to destroy themselves. I shop in the children's section and wear training bras meant for adolescent girls. During high school, I wore baggy sweaters to avoid teasing from other girls. The rumor still spread that I had an eating disorder. I didn't, but I felt like there must be something wrong with me.

Since I never ended up sprouting curves like I should have, I didn't feel like I had the right to consider myself a true woman. I certainly couldn't imagine myself in a relationship. Not because I thought I was ugly, but because my body made me exempt from attraction and anything that could lead to. I didn't know any women who actually looked like me.

Thin Women and "Real Beauty"

Recently, there has been a movement within our culture to promote "real beauty from real women." Dove's advertising campaign splashes images of smiling women of a wide range of sizes, ages and ethnicities across magazine ads and television commercials.

Thin women are not included in this "real women" movement. Why would they be? After all, thin women have plenty of representation in the media: models who starve themselves to perform as walking clothing hangers and celebrities who divulge dieting tips and check into rehab clinics. Thin women are unrealistic, a supposed ideal that no one idealizes, a source of envy and disgust.

Let's think about the real issue here:

No woman should feel like an open target when she walks down the street for any reason.

If we want young girls to stop starving or stuffing themselves, we need to celebrate women of all shapes and sizes, from petite to plus-size. We need to listen to what they tell us. We have to hold the media accountable for the way it represents women.

Too Fat, Too Thin

The potentially exciting appearance of breasts, hips, and thighs was tainted for some of the girls we talked to [in our research] by toxic comments from family members. While such comments were more common from fathers and male siblings, mothers were not immune from teasing their daughters. Several girls described being teased by their mothers as they moved through puberty and recalled nicknames they had been given like "fat stuff," "chubbo," "big mix," and "fat cat," among others. . . .

Girls were also teased for being too thin (for example, with the nickname "beanpole"). Several girls described being tormented about their weight by brothers and sisters, especially if their siblings knew it was a sensitive issue for them. Whereas some girls described acting defiant and impervious to this teasing, others ran into their rooms and cried.

Mimi Nichter, Fat Talk:
What Girls and Their Parents Say About Dieting.
Cambridge, MA: Harvard University Press, 2000.

The comments will never stop coming, even if I double my weight. There will always be people who will be disappointed in my body and tell me how I ought to change it to better suit them. When they do, as they inevitably will, I tell myself:

"Little do you know, this body ran 3 miles without stopping, operated a chainsaw, hiked mountains, travelled across four continents, comforted children in pain, held vigil for friends in pain, witnessed countless sunsets, and had more amazing sex than I can count.

"Now try and tell me my body is lacking in any way!"

The "Too" Syndrome

Too many women have the "too" syndrome, whether they perceive themselves to be too big, too short, too tall, too shy or too loud. I struggle with insecurity, but I'm learning to appreciate my body for what it can do. The more that I take care of it, the more it helps me do the things I love. This became more important to me than worrying about how others saw me. I am the one in control now.

This year, I decided to challenge my insecurities by pushing myself physically in ways that I never have before: I joined AmeriCorps (National Civilian Community Corps) to perform a year of service across the United States in the areas of education, disaster relief and the environment. Currently, I'm helping to build a boardwalk at Moundville Archaeological Park in Alabama. I carry logs twice my size, whack boards with a sledgehammer and wield a giant nail gun outside in the sun, eight hours a day, five days a week. I often want to give up and let the stronger people get the work done more efficiently, but this is something I have to do for myself. I know I'm definitely not the strongest member on my team, but learning how to trust my body is my true work.

"In fact, the real danger may be that the contrast between the girls on the catwalks and the girls at the mall is creating an atmosphere ripe for binge dieting and the kind of unhealthy eating habits that ultimately result in weight gain, not loss."

The Fashion Industry Promotes Eating Disorders

Jessica Bennett

Jessica Bennett is a senior writer at Newsweek *and the* Daily Beast. *In the following viewpoint, she argues that the trend for superthin models in the fashion industry negatively impacts eating disorders. Bennett asserts that as models become skinnier, American women become heavier and the discrepancy creates an environment that may lead to binge dieting and unhealthy eating habits, as well as factor in to the development of bulimia, anorexia, and binge eating disorder. Nevertheless, she points out, the fashion industry claims that the demands of the public dictate the gaunt body types seen on the runways and in advertisements.*

As you read, consider the following questions:

1. How much has the gap grown between the average model and the average American woman, according to Bennett?

2. How are the bodies of models and celebrities digitally manipulated, as described by Bennett?

3. How has the body become the central focus in people's lives, as claimed in the viewpoint?

The specter of dangerously thin models has raised its beautiful, lolling head once again, this time at New York's Fashion Week, which ends Friday [in February 2007]. Stung by negative publicity about boney apparitions on the catwalks, the fashion industry invited eating-disorder experts to an unprecedented symposium on the subject in the tents at Bryant Park. It was quite a spectacle. The press was regaled with tales of models living on lethally small amounts of lettuce and Diet Coke. The fashionistas declared that superthin was now "out" and promised to keep a better eye on the young waifs. But no one in the U.S. clothing biz seems eager to impose minimum weight guidelines on models, as some European shows have done. Diane von Fürstenberg, president of the Council of Fashion Designers of America (CFDA), added fuel to the fire when she recently told a reporter that model weigh-ins in New York would happen "over my dead body."

The Real Danger

While the travails of the thin and beautiful almost always make for good copy, we should remember that only about 1 percent of the American population is anorexic, while nearly two-thirds of adults are overweight or obese, according to the U.S. Centers for Disease Control and Prevention. So it's not as if skinny models have inspired an epidemic of slimness. In fact, the real danger may be that the contrast between the girls on the catwalks and the girls at the mall is creating an atmosphere ripe for binge dieting and the kind of unhealthy eating habits that ultimately result in weight gain, not loss. "You always [have to] look at the discrepancy between the real and the ideal," says Cynthia [M.] Bulik, a clinical psychologist who heads the eating-disorders program at the University of North Carolina at Chapel Hill. "If [kids] see themselves gaining weight and then they see these ultra-thin models, the discrepancy between how they see themselves in the mirror and how they feel they have to look is bigger. And that can prompt more extreme behaviors."

Unfortunately, that gap between the ordinary and the elite is growing rapidly. As American women have gotten heavier, models have gotten thinner and taller. Twenty-five years ago, the average female model weighed 8 percent less than the average American woman, according to researchers. Today, models weigh about 23 percent less than the average woman. Models are also leggier than before. Usually about 5 feet 10 inches tall, they are a good five inches taller than they were 10 years ago. Meanwhile, a typical woman is about 5 feet 4 inches and weighs 155 pounds, according to a 2004 SizeUSA study. The trend is enough to make any woman feel like a hobbit in comparison to what they're seeing in magazines.

But here's the rub: Thanks to technology, often not even the models themselves can compare to their portfolios. Increasingly, photos for print are enhanced and perfected to an astonishing degree. Not only are moles, acne and subtle facial hair erased from already pretty faces, but retouchers are routinely asked by editors and advertisers to enlarge eyes, trim normal-size ears, fill in hairlines, straighten teeth and lengthen the already-narrow necks, waists and legs of 18-year-old beauties. "We're always stretching the models' legs and slimming their thighs," says a photo retoucher who works for a high-end Manhattan agency. In some cases, hands, feet or even legs are replaced in photos when the subject's parts don't add up to a perfect whole. "Sometimes I feel a little like Frankenstein," says the retoucher, who would only speak anonymously because of the potential for professional backlash. The irony, she adds, is that the models and actresses pictured usually have already been through hours of hair styling and makeup—including body makeup—to remove the slightest blemish. Yes, you heard that right, even after all of that, a 5-foot-10, 110-pound model still does not have legs that are long or skinny enough to suit some advertisers and fashion editrixes.

One might argue that photo alteration has been around for eons, but what is new is the industry shift from film to digital media about four years ago. Now it's easier, faster and more routine to clean up and "perfect" faces and figures. The doctored images are so pervasive that our eyes are perhaps becoming too accustomed to them. "The result is a culture of kids who are being socialized to unrealistic images—who need to learn to separate the real from the fabricated," says Cornell University historian Joan Jacobs Brumberg, the author of *The Body Project*, which looks at the diaries of teenage girls from the 1820s through the 1980s. "Girls internalize this form of self-criticism and say, 'I don't look like that.' But in reality, nobody looks like that."

Fashion's Finger on the Trigger

How do these unrealistic portrayals affect the number of people with eating disorders? It's hard to say. The statistics are notoriously difficult to track because of the shame surrounding these diseases. Experts say that sufferers are influenced by a combination of genetics and environmental triggers. But even if no one factor is to blame, for some of the 10 million women and one million men in the United States who struggle with anorexia and bulimia (and the 25 million more who suffer from binge eating disorder), what they see in the media can, in some cases, have a pivotal impact. "Genes load the

gun, environment pulls the trigger—and right now the fashion industry has their finger on the trigger," says Bulik.

Particularly disturbing are indications that the quest for perfection is reaching into younger age groups. Kids form their body images almost as soon as they can form words, and girls are now thinking negatively about their shapes in grammar school. Today, 42 percent of first- to third-grade girls want to be thinner, while 81 percent of 10-year-olds are afraid of getting fat, according to a 2004 global study by the Dove "Real Beauty" campaign. "What we've seen more and more is an increasingly narrow image of beauty, not just completely defined by physical appearance, but a particular body type— tall, thin, maybe blond, with very little diversity," says Nancy Etcoff, a Harvard psychology professor and author of *Survival of the Prettiest*. The effects of that are striking. The Dove study found that just 2 percent of women and girls said they would describe themselves as beautiful, while two-thirds said they avoided basic activities on days they felt unattractive. Those activities ranged from going to the beach or a party to showing up for work or school—even voicing an opinion.

The fact that we're making the body the central focus of our lives is no accident, says Brumberg. Rather, it's "a symptom of historical changes that are only now beginning to be understood," she writes. So what are those changes? To start, there has been a century-long shift from concern for good work to concern for good looks, says Brumberg. And while in the 1920s, for example, girls started becoming conscious of celebrity culture—and, she says, for the first time using the word "image"—today's obsession with personal appearance is largely a result of the technology that allows us to focus on it. "[Technological] inventions increased our level of self-scrutiny," she says. "Mirrors, movies, scales—the modern bathroom. You have to have a certain environment for that obsessive concern."

Of course, environment affects each woman differently. Influences on body image range from our families and school to our peer groups or media consumption—even whether or not we take part in sports. For longtime model Carré Otis, that environment was fashion—and the pressure it placed on her to be thin encouraged a nearly two-decade battle with a host of unhealthy habits. Now 38 and healthy, Otis (who is 5-foot-10 and at times weighed as little as 100 pounds) says she worries about the pressures her young daughter will someday face. "We're living in a culture that's so physically oriented," she says. "It's really dangerous for young girls to operate under the assumption that models, in general, are the majority."

Fat Doesn't Sell

But the majority image isn't what the public wants these days, according to the fashion elites. "Fat doesn't sell fashion," says

Imogen Edwards-Jones, a journalist and author of *Fashion Babylon*, an insider's look at the industry. "People don't fantasize about being a size 16—they fantasize about being a size 8." So even if the public can't fit into (much less afford) a size 0 designer dress, they'll probably buy a magazine with a size 0 model wearing that dress. "It's a presentation of this fantasy, and you buy into that," says Steven Kolb, the executive director of CFDA.

Of course, that can always change. Curves were cool in the '80s (remember [model] Cindy Crawford?) and '90s ([model] Anna Nicole Smith). And the industry will likely swing back around to embrace them again. Already, the faces on the catwalks in New York this week are looking somewhat less gaunt. But it doesn't look like it's going to get any easier for women to convince themselves, or their daughters, to stop looking for the model in the mirror.

"And are women really so pathologically stupid that they are unable to distinguish the fantasy of the runway from the realities of their own bodies?"

The Fashion Industry Should Not Be Held Responsible for Eating Disorders

Lisa Hilton

In the following viewpoint, Lisa Hilton refutes the criticisms that models are too thin and the fashion industry encourages eating disorders. Similar to athletes, top models show exemplary professionalism and discipline to maintain their figures, she states, and it is hypocritical that men's sports are never scrutinized for their weight qualifications and extreme dieting methods. Furthermore, Hilton persists that the prevalence of anorexia is very low, especially compared to the obesity epidemic in Great Britain and the United States. The author is a British writer and contributes to Vogue *and the* Sunday Telegraph.

As you read, consider the following questions:

1. What does Sasha claim about being a former model under the pressure to be thin?

Lisa Hilton, "What's Wrong with Skinny?," thedailybeast.com, February 8, 2010. Reproduced by permission.

2. What methods of weight loss are commonly used in men's sports, as stated by the author?

3. How does Hilton respond to the argument that models now are statistically thinner than the average woman than they were in the past?

Another spring, another show season. In the mercurial world of fashion, it's comforting to know that some things will never change—[*Vogue* editor in chief] Anna Wintour's hairdo, an Olsen [referring to actress Mary-Kate or Ashley] in the front row, and a tsunami of earnest media coverage on how a conspiracy of evil designers and foolish models are reducing women to jutting-collarboned wrecks, barely able to lift their heads from the lavatory bowl to make it to Barneys in time for the pre-collections.

Let's be clear. Anorexia and bulimia are horrific psychological conditions, destroying lives and families, and carrying devastating long-term health risks even when not fatal. Sufferers deserve nothing but respect and support for their condition. But is that condition nearly so prevalent as the barrage of attention it regularly attracts actually deserves? And are women really so pathologically stupid that they are unable to distinguish the fantasy of the runway from the realities of their own bodies? Arguably, the "size zero" debate is merely another side of the infantilized, hysterical box women thought they had clawed their way out of a century ago, an insidious means of suggesting that though we can run companies and governments we're still not quite rational creatures, too dainty and delicate to cope with the dissonances between the Bambi-limbed aspirations of the catwalk and our own wretched, cellulite-smothered carcasses.

Skinniness Is Professionally Necessary

That women can be beautiful at any size, age, or color is something no serious person would dispute. But the fashion industry is ultimately unconcerned with beauty; its objective is selling clothes, and the consensus remains that in order to achieve this, models need to be thin. Whether or not this is aesthetically desirable is a matter of taste, not morality. The recent success of "bigger" girls such as [models] Lara Stone or Daisy Lowe suggests that it does not always obtain, as *V* magazine's recent billboard campaign emphasizes. Even [designer] Karl Lagerfeld has jumped onboard the biscuits and gravy train with his latest shoot of Miss Dirty Martini. The fact remains that for girls chasing the big money, skinniness is professionally necessary.

I spoke to one ex-model, Sasha*, who in her heyday walked for [designers] Tom Ford and [John] Galliano; "Sure, we had to be skinny. I lived on Diet Coke and apples for two years. For the couture, we had to get up at 4 a.m. to be sewn into the clothes and there was huge pressure to be thin. But I made a million dollars by the time I was 20, I bought a town house in Manhattan and put myself through Columbia. Does that make me a victim?" For every Sasha, there are a hundred hungry wannabes who fall by the wayside, but why are we so keen to dismiss the professionalism and discipline of models who are prepared to make sacrifices to reach the top? Is it a coincidence that modeling is the one profession outside the porn industry where women consistently out-earn their male counterparts? Are we just a bit angry that young women with no qualifications other than what nature gave them get to be so powerful?

We rarely get hysterical about the weight qualifications required of male sportsmen. Jockeys, boxers, and wrestlers put themselves through torture to make weight. A survey published by the U.S. National Library of Medicine lists a range of weight-loss methods for jockeys that would make any model agency proud—69 percent skip meals, 34 percent use diuretics, 67 percent sweat off the pounds in the sauna, 30 percent

* not her real name

regularly vomit and 40 percent use laxatives. So where are the angry headlines and government initiatives to fatten up our jockeys? Perhaps in sport, the sacrifices are viewed as noble, and the rewards (prize money or prestigious college scholarships) seen as secondary to the noble end of winning for its own sake. Shifting dresses is after all a frivolous little multibillion-dollar industry. Or is it that men are considered psychologically robust enough to admire the buff beauties of *GQ* or *Men's Health* without getting their tighty-whities in a twist? Women, it is implied, are too fragile to make a distinction between the Victoria's Secret catalogue and their own closets. Young women who choose to conform to the demands of their industry in order to maximize their earnings are portrayed as irrational and deluded, while young men who make comparable choices are admired.

Eating Disorders Are Not on the Rise

Eating disorders, we are told, are on the rise, ready to grab the gut of any vulnerable teenager who spends too much time dreaming over *Vogue*. Except, actually, they're not.

The South Carolina Department of Mental Health claims that one in 200 American women suffer from anorexia, as opposed to the American Heart Association's statistic of 39.4 million women suffering from obesity. So that's half a percent against 34 percent. *MJA*, the medical journal of Australia, concurs with the 0.5 percent statistic, noting that *anorexia nervosa* is not common and adding, "Eating disorders have captured the public imagination. . . . This publicity tends to obscure the continuing puzzle created by these . . . conditions." Clinical Knowledge Summaries 2009, the statistics department of the British National Institute for Health and Clinical Excellence, says that 19 out of one million women are diagnosed as anorexic, as opposed to 240,000 per million for obesity. The British NHS [National Health Service] survey of disordered eating noted 620 hospital treatments for anorexia or bulimia (with

Not Merely Linked to Fashion

In common discourse, anorexia is often viewed as a response to the pressure to be thin operated by the media. I have argued that the (omni) presence of ultrathin models does not explain the disorder. It rather shows that in our society (Western society) we are attracted to thinness. This raises the question as to why we are attracted to thinness.

Many people believe that this attraction to thinness is a contemporary phenomenon.... [The] dread of fat was common in previous eras and ... the straitjacket of diet has for a long time been considered an imperative for women.

The attraction to thinness is not a phenomenon merely linked to "fashion". Thinness *becomes* valuable in a determined sociocultural context, for what it symbolises. In the sociocultural context of the Western world, it symbolises the submission of the body to the mind.

Michael Freeman, ed.
Children's Health and Children's Rights.
Boston, MA: Martinus Nijhoff Publishers, 2006.

some patients registered twice or more) for 2005 to 2006 as opposed to 17,458 for the same period for obesity.

There is simply no argument to be had as to the most prevalent weight-related threat to young women's health, and yet still every year someone vilifies poor old [model] Kate Moss for suggesting that nothing tastes as good as skinny feels. Well, right on, Kate. The hoary old trope that models are statistically thinner than the average woman now as opposed to 20 years ago proves nothing more than that the average woman got heavier.

Blurring the Difference Between Harmless Fad and Genuine Disease

Women have always gone to absurd and often dangerous extremes in pursuit of the beauty myth. Fourteen-inch waists and mercury-eaten complexions for the Elizabethans, phthisis-inducing sponged muslin for Romantic groupies. One of the many rather creepy truisms trotted out in support of "real" models is that much fashion is produced by men who would prefer us to resemble adolescent boys. Yeah, we *get* that. Fashion is about fantasy, about impossibility, about, dare we say it, art. Most women can tell the difference. The suffragettes got us the vote and they did it in whalebone corsets. Stop the presses, how we look is not actually who we are.

Women recovering from severe eating disorders consistently report that their illness was not induced by the desire to look like [model] Gisele [Bündchen], but by far more complex psychological issues. Is it not demeaning to insist that such women were gripped by nothing more than vanity? Feminism has created a world in which young women are safe and secure enough to do a lot of stupid things as part of a rite of passage—they can drink Jell-O shots and worship [actor] Robert Pattinson and grow up to become accountants or lawyers or CEOs [chief executive officers]. Laying off the Krispy Kremes for a few years in order to shimmy into Paige jeans is hardly on a par with being unable to menstruate, but the rhetoric of the eating-disorder lobby insultingly blurs the difference between harmless faddiness and genuine disease.

Thin is a feminist issue because it grabs the headlines from more serious causes with which committed feminists might concern themselves. As the late great [comedian] George Carlin put it, "What kind of goddamn disease is this anyway? 'I don't wanna eat!', 'Well, go f--- yourself.'" If we want to worry about malnutrition, why don't we get exercised about the hundreds of thousands of women who starve slowly around the world? Thin is a feminist issue because the well-meant anxiety over eating disorders makes us look dim. It's patronizing and disempowering and reduces legitimate concerns over body issues to juvenile whining. We could just leave the models to get on with their job. Maybe the radical way to look at this season's shows would be to enjoy the spectacle, buy the frock and get on with something more interesting? Obviously, we're not all brainless enough to starve ourselves out of existence because a sinister conglomerate of designers and editors says we should. Sadly, the current correlation between fashion and anorexia suggests precisely that.

> "The intricate dance of genes and environment influences how at risk each of us is to succumbing to urges to binge."

Binge Eating Is Linked to Genetic and Environmental Factors

Cynthia M. Bulik

Cynthia M. Bulik is a professor in the Department of Psychiatry, nutrition professor in the School of Public Health, and director of the eating disorders program at the University of North Carolina at Chapel Hill. In the following viewpoint, excerpted from her book Crave: Why You Binge Eat and How to Stop, *Bulik asserts that genes and the environment are linked to the development of binge eating. Bulik states that extensive studies on twins demonstrate that the chances of genetically inheriting the disorder are proportionately high. In addition, Bulik proposes that environmental factors, such as behaviors in the home and shifts in society and culture, can trigger binge eating.*

As you read, consider the following questions:

1. What is the heritability of binge eating, according to a 2004 study in which Bulik participated?

2. What is a "double disadvantage," as described by Bulik?

3. How does the author explain how body dissatisfaction and disordered eating appear among girls in Fiji?

Current studies seem to conclude that your hardwiring determines how vulnerable you are to the pernicious behaviors encouraged by the food, fashion, and entertainment industries. Whether the pressure comes from the fashion industry's emphasis on exaggerated thinness or television makeover shows that promise that you, too, can achieve perfection, the extreme dieting that may result can boomerang until your body finally gives in and screams "Feed me!"

Hardwired to Binge

While another woman with a different genetic profile might be able to diet and then return to reasonable eating, the physical and psychological deprivation that follows an extreme diet can set off an uncontrollable binge in a woman genetically inclined to binge eating disorder. Let us take a moment here to examine just how our genetic makeup can make it seem like we're literally hardwired to binge.

Before birth, each of us gets a set of chromosomes with genes that influence everything from hair texture to skin color to the risk for certain diseases and disorders. In the past ten years or so, a rash of scientific studies has begun to make it clear that eating disorders such as anorexia and bulimia nervosa run in families. Other studies have shown that obesity is even more closely linked within families.

But only recently have studies comparing families and twins revealed that binge eating disorder can also be an inherited trait passed along from parents to children. As with all genetically influenced disorders, binge eating disorder does not get passed along to every sibling. Unlike single-gene diseases such as Huntington's (if you have the gene, you get the disease), syndromes like binge eating disorder are influenced by many genes and many environmental factors. Even though Kathy and her slimmer sister Barbara have 50 percent of their genes in common (as do all siblings), their risk for binge eating disorder might be quite different. Still, the evidence is fairly clear that family members of someone with binge eating disorder are over twice as likely to suffer from binge eating disorder themselves—just like having a family history of heart disease or diabetes.

Over the past twenty years, researchers in genetic epidemiology, including myself, have combed through countless family profiles to show that eating disorders track through the generations. We learned that relatives of people with anorexia and bulimia are seven to twelve times at higher risk for an eating disorder—about the same rate as the risk for inheriting a tendency toward bipolar disorder and schizophrenia. Researchers have also learned that binge eating disorder runs in families.

However, family studies have a limitation: They can tell us if a trait runs in a family, but they can't tell us why. It could be because someone has inherited genes that influence a disorder, but it could also be because a child witnessed binge eating in a parent and learned those behaviors through a process called modeling—just the way you might learn how to swing a baseball bat from watching your dad play softball. So family studies can't separate genetic influences from environmental ones.

Twin Studies

The best way to identify whether there is a genetic component is with twin and adoption studies. Identical twins are basically clones—for most intents and purposes, they share identical sets of genes. Genetically speaking, fraternal twins are no different than regular siblings. Like Kathy and Barbara, they share 50 percent of their genes, but unlike Kathy and Barbara, they grew up in the same environment (starting with their shared time in the womb). So the only thing that differs between identical and fraternal twins is the percentage of genes they have in common.

Let's consider an example. My first child was born when we lived in an apartment in Pittsburgh, Pennsylvania, in the winter. He was born into a family of two adults. My third child was born in the summer in Christchurch, New Zealand. She was born into a family of two adults and two children. Not only were they born on different continents in different seasons, they were also born into different families. Even the food that was available to me during the pregnancies differed dramatically. My children share 50 percent of their genes, but they were exposed to very different environments even before birth. Since twins develop together in the womb and are born into the same family at the same time, they share their environmental legacy.

Since the only difference between identical and fraternal twins is the percentage of genes they share, twin studies are able to isolate genetic from environmental factors by comparing how much more similar identical twins are than fraternal twins. If, for example, in a large sample of twins, you find that both members of identical twin pairs have binge eating disorder more frequently than both members of fraternal twin pairs, it suggests that genes might be involved.

So, how do twin studies work? The basic premise is that individuals vary—in height, in our cholesterol levels, and in whether we have binge eating disorder or not. What twin studies allow us to do is to place estimates on *why* we vary—an estimate of how much is due to genes and how much is due to environment. The proportion that is due to genes is known as *heritability*.

In 1998 I was part of a group of researchers who reported that based on data about thousands of sets of twins, the heritability of the symptom of binge eating could be estimated to be somewhere between 46 and 82 percent. Next, several Norwegian researchers and I wanted to move this estimate beyond looking at just the symptom of binge eating and closer to truly understanding how much genes contributed to binge eating disorder. To do this, we turned to a sample of over eight thousand sets of same-sex and opposite-sex twins in a Norwegian registry to see how much genes and environment contribute to the actual binge eating syndrome.

Linkage Studies

Our study, published in 2004, confirmed that the syndrome of binge eating disorder also appeared to have a substantial genetic component. For both women and men with the disorder, the heritability was around 47 percent. Family studies tell us that the disorder runs in families, and twin studies tell us that genetic factors influence why the disorder runs in families, but neither of those types of studies tells us which genes we are talking about, where they are, or how they work. So the field has moved forward, to developing techniques that allow us to identify the genes and what they do. With the completion of the Human Genome Project, by 2003 more than twenty-four thousand genes in human DNA have been identified.

In linkage studies, we try to narrow the search for culprit genes to particular areas on particular chromosomes. It sometimes astonishes people to hear that for eating disorders—which have been considered to be largely cultural phenomena for decades—we have identified areas on the genome where these risk genes might lie. We have made a lot of progress in linking certain traits on certain chromosomes to anorexia nervosa and bulimia nervosa, and studies on binge eating disorder are not far behind.

The Delicate Dance of Genes and Environment

Fighting the tendency to binge eat is a psychological struggle that pits your rational mind against your biology. But it's not all due to genes—your environment also plays an important role in your relationship with food. The intricate dance of genes and environment influences how at risk each of us is to succumbing to urges to binge.

Teasing out genetic factors from environmental ones is tricky business, in part because under most conditions the same people who give you your genes (your parents) also provide you with the environment in which you are raised. A classic example is IQ. Children of high IQ parents are more likely to have high IQs than children whose parents have lower IQs. Even though we know that intelligence is inherited, there is a hitch. Parents who are smart also tend to provide their children with rich and stimulating environments. They are the ones who buy Baby Mozart tapes, read to their children, and supply stimulating toys, so their kids have a "double advantage." They inherited genes for intelligence, but they were also exposed to an environment that stimulated their minds.

Unfortunately the opposite scenario can happen as well—instead of a double advantage, children can get a double disadvantage. For example, a child who inherits the risk for binge eating disorder might also grow up watching Mom and Dad restrict calories at dinner, then eat their way through a bag of cookies an hour later. Not only might the child have increased genetic risk, she or he also has been exposed to unhealthy eating habits, maybe never learning what a healthy portion size or a normal eating schedule is.

[Take, for example, the experience of] Tish whose father once offered her five dollars for every pound she lost in grade school. Turns out her father was bulimic for much of her formative years. Recalling a period when she was growing up and lived with her father, Tish describes how every night after dinner he would put down his fork, invite Tish for a walk across their property, pick an orange from one of their many orange trees, and after a few slices, make himself throw up before walking back home.

At the time, of course, Tish thought nothing of it; she had no barometer to tell her whether this was normal or abnormal behavior. Today, of course, she realizes her own eating disorder is linked closely to her father's. I don't know whether the link is genetic or environmental, although I personally suspect it's a classic case of a double disadvantage.

One study we did looked at the way in which mothers with eating disorders fed their babies and toddlers. Normally moms (and dads!) go to all sorts of crazy lengths to get their children to engage in eating—making faces, playing games, singing songs, opening their mouths as the spoon gets closer to the baby's mouth. It is an emotionally engaging, interactive experience.

But that's not true of many mothers with eating disorders. When we videotaped how they fed their kids, all that came across was stress and anxiety. There was no facial expression, no engagement with their children. It was perfectly clear that eating was an uncomfortable act for them. Mealtimes were tense.

In the case of these mothers with eating disorders, the result is that adults with dysregulated eating often have difficulty knowing what healthy, normal eating is for their children. Even though as parents we're supposed to model healthy eating, if we have difficulty doing it for ourselves, we're in a tough spot when trying to teach our children. But with help, the cycle can be broken—even children who are genetically predisposed to binge eating disorder don't have to fall into the same eating traps as their parents. . . .

Binge Eating and Cultural Environments

What happens when there is a rapid and extreme shift in the environment? In recent years with the globalization of both the food and the entertainment industries, cultures that previously have been isolated from the bombardment of fast food and our culturally sanctioned thin ideal have become barraged by excess calories, fat, sugar, and images already widespread in the Western world. As you might expect, the results aren't pretty.

Whereas the shift was relatively gradual for us (Kentucky Fried Chicken and McDonald's arrived in the 1950s, and nowadays most suburban turnpikes are literally lined with fast-food establishments), many other countries—especially in Asia and Eastern Europe—got a rapid influx of many such establishments. (Merely eleven years after the first set of golden arches appeared on the Ginza in 1971, McDonald's became the biggest restaurant chain in Japan.)

The same was true for the cultural "thin ideal" in the international fashion industry. We first encountered the ninety-one-pound Twiggy, arguably the first supermodel, in 1966, and she was an anomaly. But then gradually the thin ideal became the norm, leading to the chic trend of the 1990s and frank emaciation by the 2000s.

Along with these changes in the environment, in the United States we saw an increase in both obesity and eating disorders. But these changes occurred over the course of just a few generations. Since our gene pool can't change that fast (it takes many many generations to see changes in the gene pool), what you are seeing is how changes in the environment can lead to different expressions of genes that have been there all along.

The Girls of Fiji

Let's take Fiji as an example. Dr. Anne Becker of Harvard University conducted a telling study on the island. She first studied girls' eating habits on Fiji in 1988 and then returned in 1995. By 1998 she had visited again and this time found a sharp rise in disordered eating behaviors and body dissatisfaction among those girls.

What had happened in the interim? Television made its way to the island. In her 1998 survey, taken thirty-eight months after TV arrived on Nadroga, Fiji, 11.3 percent of girls, aged seventeen on average, reported that they had vomited to control weight in comparison to 0 percent who reported this behavior in 1995. Plus, 29 percent of schoolgirls scored high on an eating disorders test in comparison to 13 percent in 1995.

Showing the power of the tube, in 1998, 74 percent of the Fijian girls reported feeling "too big or fat." And if they watched TV at least three nights per week, they were 50 percent more likely to see themselves as too fat, and 30 percent more likely to diet. A full 62 percent of Fijian high school girls in 1998 reported dieting in the past month, which is astonishing in a culture that historically has valued voluptuous bodies and generous feeding. Girls with rounded Pacific Islander bodies suddenly wanted to be thin and svelte. What shows were they watching? *Melrose Place* and *Beverly Hills, 90210*, among others. So the genes that influenced risk for these behaviors were there all along, but they may have been unleashed by environmental triggers such as the images of [actresses] Heather Locklear and Tori Spelling.

Genes work in many ways, including making you more sensitive to the people and places in your environment. Some people can walk around in a daze, oblivious of the world around them. Nothing penetrates their protective shell and environmental insults bounce off them like water off a duck's back. Others are more like emotional Velcro. Environmental triggers stick in their craw; they carry them around and have difficulty shaking them loose. Environmental insults get under their skin like a nasty splinter.

Periodical and Internet Sources Bibliography

The following articles have been selected to supplement the diverse views presented in this chapter.

Laura Bond "Ban on 'Skeletal' Models Does Not Fix Society's Obsession with Thinness," *University Echo*, February 8, 2007.

Cynthia Bulik "Genetic Risk Factor for Eating Disorders," *Eating Disorders Recovery Today*, Fall 2007.

Susan Daly "Now They're Airbrushing the Cover Girls Bigger," *Irish Independent*, June 17, 2009.

Emily Deans "Dieting Can Make You Lose Your Mind," *Evolutionary Psychiatry* (blog), March 24, 2011. www.psychologytoday.com.

Vivian Diller "Is Photoshop Destroying America's Body Image?," *Huffington Post*, July 7, 2011. www.huffingtonpost.com.

Steven Erlanger "Point, Shoot, Retouch and Label?," *New York Times*, December 2, 2009.

Abby Gillies "Dark Disorder That Preys on Perfection," *New Zealand Herald*, July 17, 2011.

Melissa Healy "Binge Eating: Is It a Form of Addiction?," *Los Angeles Times*, November 23, 2009.

Naomi Jefferies "Eating Disorders: A Psychological Approach," *Psychology Review*, November 2007.

Libby Rodenbough "Killer Fashion: An Industry in Denial," *In These Times*, March 28, 2011.

CHAPTER 3

What Role Does the Internet Play in Eating Disorders?

Chapter Preface

Jemima Owens insists that blogging about her anorexia was important to her recovery. Hospitalized for the eating disorder from fifteen to eighteen years old, the British woman felt alienated when she was released. "I could not relate to 'normal' people my own age, and as my weight started to drop again I barely had enough energy to get through a day at school, let alone socialise afterwards," Owens told the *Guardian*, in a March 2011 interview. Her anorexia took a toll on her home life as well. "[M]y brother was too embarrassed by his 'mental' sister to have friends back to the house, and my parents and I rowed constantly over food as they desperately tried to prevent another relapse," she continued. Starting her blog, in which she posted daily for a year, provided an emotional outlet. "Blogging allowed me to articulate my struggles and triumphs away from the fractious environment of the dinner table," Owens asserted. Also, she found tough love and support from readers and even her parents, who left comments such as "how proud I am of my beautiful daughter."

However, for Stephanie Moore, another British woman, her anorexia spiraled out of control on the Internet. As a member on a pro-anorexia website, she documented her harrowing weight loss for hundreds of followers, sharing photos of her emaciated body and advice on starvation. "Looking back at the fact I gave 'thinspiration' tips to other girls makes me feel bad," she explained to the *Sun*, in March 2010. "I used to visit some of the sites I used and post, 'I'm pro-recovery now.' I hoped it would help and in some way undo the terrible things I had done." Now, Moore warns women to avoid those sites without compromise: "I would tell girls who are dragged into thinspiration to get out of there as soon as possible, delete everything from your computer, and talk to the people who you are closest to."

In the following chapter, the authors debate the role the Internet plays in eating disorders.

"If ever there was an example of words that could kill, a 'pro-ana' or 'pro-mia' website could be a contender."

Pro-Ana Websites Are Dangerous

Lauren Cox

Lauren Cox reports for the ABC medical news unit. In the following viewpoint, she writes that many websites claiming to offer support for individuals with eating disorders actually promote anorexia ("pro-ana") or bulimia ("pro-mia"). A recent study, the author states, reveals that over 80 percent of 180 active pro-ana and pro-mia sites advocating recovery provide harmful advice on how to maintain an eating disorder and images of bony models for "thinspiration." As a result, these mixed messages contribute to the ambiguity that sufferers of eating disorders have toward treatment and overcoming their illness, Cox explains.

As you read, consider the following questions:

1. What kind of "elitist" language is used to describe eating disorders on pro-ana and pro-mia sites, as given in the viewpoint?

Lauren Cox, "Pro-Anorexia Websites Send Convoluted and Deadly Messages, Study Finds," abcnews.go.com, June 17, 2010. Reproduced by permission.

2. As stated by Cox, what do psychiatrists claim about the paradox of recovery and encouragement of eating disorders on pro-ana sites?

3. According to Cox, what advice do psychiatrists offer parents since most eating disorders develop during adolescence?

If ever there was an example of words that could kill, a "pro-ana" or "pro-mia" website could be a contender. "Ana" stands for anorexia and just as the name implies, the "pro-ana" and "pro-mia" (for bulimia) websites encourage starving yourself and explain how to do it. Johanna [S.] Kandel, 31, said she used to read memoirs of anorexics to feed her obsession with losing weight. Now nine years after her decade-long battle with anorexia, she sees the same inclinations in people visiting "pro-ana" sites. "It's making it a lot more accessible, not only to get tips . . . they actually get supported by one another to become more engrossed in their eating disorder," said Kandel, who founded the Alliance for Eating Disorders Awareness.

"Although you feel [you] cannot recover, you absolutely can and you deserve to," said Kandel. Anorexia nervosa has the highest mortality rate of any psychiatric illness. Between 5 to 10 percent of individuals with anorexia will die within 10 years of the onset of the disorder, according to the National Association of Anorexia Nervosa and Associated Disorders.

Psychiatrists are so worried by pro-ana sites, they would rather not see news about them at all. But the sites are so pervasive that doctors feel they must visit and study them to treat patients. A new study that looked at 180 active pro-ana and pro-mia sites found convoluted messages of alluring emotional support and deadly advice. As expected, 83 percent of the 180 sites openly advised visitors on how to start or continue an eating disorder, according to the study published today in the *American Journal of Public Health*. Obvious instructions, such as BMI [body mass index] calculators and calorie counters were common, but so was indirect encouragement. Eighty-five percent of the sites included "Thinspiration" sections meant to visually encourage eating disorders through pictures of bony models. Connie Diekman, director of university nutrition at Washington University in St. Louis, estimated that 1 to 3 percent of all women will become anorexic at some point in their lives and 2 to 8 percent of all women will become bulimic at some point in their lives.

Anorexia—Rare but Deadly

Diekman, who is the immediate past president of the American Dietetic Association, estimated that 2 to 5 percent of men have eating disorders. "A lot of these websites get struck down, but then they pop up elsewhere," said Dina L.G. Borzekowski, lead author of the study and associate professor at the Johns Hopkins Bloomberg School of Public Health.

Borzekowski said the general population may find the sites "extreme" and dismiss them, but from the point of view of a vulnerable teenager with a disorder, the sites could look enticing. Trouble comes, Borzekowski said, when "someone's frequenting these sites, and getting their social support from these websites."

Almost one-third of the sites in the study used "elitist" language to describe the eating disorders, as if having the mental disorder was a special privilege. Researchers cited a polite example as "If you are looking to become anorexic or become bulimic by being here then please leave" and a rude example as "IF YOU WANT TO LOSE WEIGHT, GO ON A DIET FATTY. ONE IS EITHER ANA/MIA, OR NOT. IT IS A GIFT AND YOU CANNOT DECIDE TO HAVE AN EATING DISORDER. SO IF YOU ARE LOOKING FOR A WAY TO LOSE WEIGHT, S-S-S-SORRY JUNIOR!! MOVE ON, TRY JENNY CRAIG."

At the same time, the researchers at Stanford and Johns Hopkins Universities found attempts to give support within the "ana" and "mia" sites.

Forty-two percent of the sites they studied provided venues for artistic expression, such as poetry, artwork, music and videos. Additionally, 38 percent of the sites included information on how to get help, along with recovery-oriented information.

Psychiatrists said that paradox of recovery and encouragement in pro-ana websites shows how even the most ill understand that the condition is dangerous.

"Even on these sites, there's an implication that it's not healthy," said Dr. B. Timothy Walsh at Columbia University Medical Center.

Websites Complicate Accepting Anorexia as a Disease

"One of the complicated features in treating individuals with eating disorders is . . . ambivalence about recovery," said Walsh's colleague, Dr. Evelyn Attia.

"When someone suffers from depression, they're quite clear that they would prefer experiencing life without depression," she said.

But with eating disorders, Attia said, "for many folks, even those who pursue treatment, there's often a flirtation with not getting better."

"Often patients explain just how tricky the experience of encountering these sites is. There's a part of them that wants treatment yet there are these complicated messages out there," said Attia, a member of the American Psychiatric Association and director of the center for eating disorders at Columbia University Medical Center and Weill Cornell Medical College in New York City.

The Ten Pro-Ana Commandments

1. If you aren't thin you aren't attractive.

2. Being thin is more important than being healthy.

3. You must buy clothes, cut your hair, take laxatives, starve yourself, do anything to make yourself look thinner.

4. Thou shall not eat without feeling guilty.

5. Thou shall not eat fattening food without punishing oneself afterwards.

6. Thou shall count calories and restrict intake accordingly.

7. What the scale says is the most important thing.

8. Losing weight is good/gaining weight is bad.

9. You can never be too thin.

10. Being thin and not eating are signs of true willpower and success.

Janelle Brown, "The Winner Dies,"
Salon, July 23, 2001. www.salon.com.

Psychiatrists who treat anorexia said they are anecdotally all too familiar with these sites. Yet not much research has been done on the topic or how to combat the influence of pro-ana and pro-mia sites.

"Almost every single child I get over the age of 13 has been on at least one of them, or knows all about them, even if they haven't been on them," said Dr. Stephanie Setliff, medical director at the pediatric eating disorders program at Children's Medical Center in Dallas, Texas.

"The younger children under the age of 12 aren't on them as much, because parents are monitoring their Internet use," she said.

Setliff said her approach to treating young children hasn't been to ignore the sites. Instead, she said she views them as just one more negative influence that must be addressed.

"You can't pretend that they aren't there, so then you might as well engage the treatment as part of that [the sites]," she said.

She said it is similar to the fact that "teenagers now are a generation of children who have never not seen a Photoshopped photo in magazines," said Setliff, who is an associate professor at the University of Texas Southwestern Medical Center.

Dr. David Herzog, a child psychiatrist at Harvard Medical School and Massachusetts General Hospital, said he actually does not hear of many eating disorder patients who visit these sites.

"I've occasionally heard about them. But for the most part patients don't report to me that they access those sites," said Herzog. "And I do see a fair number of eating disorder patients, and I inquire."

Herzog said while he absolutely doesn't endorse the sites, he does think it's useful to study them.

"I do try to understand what draws people to these sites so that we might be able to apply that to other sites that can draw them to healthier places," said Herzog, who is a member of the American Academy of Child and Adolescent Psychiatry.

"If we don't try to understand that, we're missing something," he said.

Parents Can Help Teen Daughters at Risk

Since the majority of people with an eating disorder develop it in the teenage years, psychiatrists say parents should be aware of their own influence over their child's behavior online and in the home.

"Monitor kids online. Know where they're going, know who they're talking to and what sites they're visiting, and if you have to put limits on computer use, do it," said Leslie Sim, a Mayo Clinic psychologist.

Sim said many children with eating disorders weren't inspired by recovery sites online either. It seemed their desire to get better fluctuated from day to day, meal to meal.

"They really require parents to do anything they can to get these kids to eat and maintain weight," said Sim. "They just need parents to take over."

Kandel said she pays attention to signs that others are looking for a way to further their eating disorder behavior. For example, when someone asks about her "lightest weight," she'll say, "the day I was born" so the person can't use the number as a way to compete in an eating disorder.

"I can understand that people who are struggling, they feel that they are in a community of people who understand," said Kandel. "But what they need to know is that on the pro-recovery side, there will be many people who understand."

> *"To its thousands of loyal members—who are all female except for one or two men—support groups are completely distinct from pro-ana sites."*

Some Eating Disorders Websites Offer Support

Jaclyn Gallucci

In the following viewpoint, Jaclyn Gallucci suggests that some online support groups for eating disorders distinguish themselves from pro-anorexia ("pro-ana") and pro-bulimia ("pro-mia") websites. Unlike pro-ana sites, she states, they strictly prohibit teaching, providing tips, and encouraging dangerous weight loss practices. Gallucci further maintains that compared to recovery sites, support sites are not judgmental, allow members to freely discuss their eating disorder behaviors, and connect individuals who have no plan for recovery to others of the same mind. Nonetheless, the author points out that some former members are conflicted over whether these sites are helpful or harmful. Gallucci is a writer for the Long Island Press.

Jaclyn Gallucci, "Not Pro-Ana: Inside the Online Sisterhood of Eating Disorders," *Long Island Press*, December 2, 2010. Copyright © 2011 Long Island Press. Reproduced by permission of the author.

As you read, consider the following questions:

1. How does the author describe pro-ana and pro-mia sites?

2. As told by the author, what happened to a photo gallery on a support site when a member asked a question about calorie intake?

3. What aspects of support sites allow members to form relationships and tight bonds, according to Gallucci?

It's 6 a.m. and Rachel is on mile five.

At 5'2" and 87 pounds she is at least 20 lbs. underweight by medical standards, but she's only halfway through her morning exercise routine.

"When someone says, 'I'm starving,' or 'I haven't eaten all day,' and you know you saw them have a piece of chocolate in the morning and all I've had was water for the past two days, it makes me enraged," she says.

On the Internet other girls admire her profile picture. It was taken on an angle under a bright light that makes her blond hair and blue eyes almost reflective and her skin a perfect even tone of unearthly white.

She looks like an angel, they say.

But that picture doesn't show the bald spots on Rachel's head where her hair is falling out, nor does it show the thick hair that is growing on her arms or how cold her skin feels. It doesn't show her brittle nails or the bite marks on her hand, the cavities in her teeth or the bruises on her body that just seem to appear out of nowhere.

For Rachel, 18, there is no upcoming event that is luring her onto the treadmill so early in the morning. There is no dress she has to fit into, no boy she is trying to impress—just the insinuation that there might be makes her very, very angry.

She's an honor student in her first year of college, who, on average, spends more than 40 hours with a second family she has never met face-to-face. Rachel has been a regular member of an online eating-disorder support group for the past three years, along with more than 4,000 other members of all ages, but mostly in their teens and early 20s, from nearly every part of the world. It's run by seven people and divided into sections by topic like "Fasting" or "Binging."

Eating-disorder-related sites have been growing steadily over the past decade—a 2007 study by Optenet, a Web security firm, showed a 470 percent increase in these sites over the course of one year—ever since they first began appearing on talk shows like *The Oprah Winfrey Show* in the late '90s.

Pro-anorexia (pro-ana) websites are those that promote anorexic behavior, where members freely exchange tips like how to purge. They are often portrayed by the media as secretive, cult-like, militant groups who worship photos of models and celebrities altered into, literally, skeletal figures; with creeds that include rules on eating similar to the 10 Commandments and a commitment to a disorder that borders on religion and rituals rivaling torture methods.

"A Support Group"

But the site Rachel belongs to "isn't like that," she says. It's considered a "support group." And to its thousands of loyal members—who are all female except for one or two men—support groups are completely distinct from pro-ana sites.

"Pro-ana sites don't care about you," says Rachel. "You can go there, and they will teach you how to be a great anorexic or the best way to throw up. That isn't allowed at my site. We won't teach you anything, and if it looks like you are here trolling for diet tips, you get kicked out."

Support sites distinguish themselves from pro-ana sites by implementing strict rules against teaching, exchanging tips and promoting outright dangerous behaviors. And they distinguish themselves from recovery sites—sites for those trying to overcome their eating disorders—by not being judgmental, allowing open talk about eating-disorder behaviors and allowing people who may have no plans of recovery to meet others who are like-minded.

With mounting pressure from recovery sites and medical professionals, both Yahoo! and GeoCities now refuse to host sites they believe glamorize eating disorders. But this often doesn't include eating-disorder sites considered support groups. Although to medical professionals and eating-disorder associations, the differences between the two are merely semantics—the difference between using the word "tips" or the word "advice" and any real differences aren't significant, except in the eyes of those with the disorder.

"These sites provide no useful information on treatment but instead encourage and falsely support those who, sadly, are ill but do not seek help," the National Eating Disorders Association warns. "Media coverage of pro-ana often triggers the already-anorexic by mentioning weights and calorie counts and by showing photographs of thin people."

We have purposely left out the names and details of the sites discussed, as well as their user names, because every person interviewed for this story found these websites through the media. . . .

But for many who visit regularly, these sites provide a special meeting place where they can find friends, all over the world, who understand them, no questions asked.

Social Networking

Sarah is a 34-year-old woman with two kids; she's a highly respected college professor with two master's degrees and a doctorate—and a husband who has no idea that his wife has a second life online. Sarah is Rachel's best friend on the site. They met on the same message board two years ago. But

Sarah's husband doesn't know Rachel exists. He also doesn't know that Sarah has had an eating disorder, in varying forms, since she was in high school.

"He doesn't even know I have any type of food issues," says Sarah. "He knows I diet, but nothing serious, which it isn't—I'm not even underweight. And I still get my period. And I only purge maybe twice a week." And many of those who frequent this site, feel the same way because they don't meet the diagnostic criteria of having either anorexia or bulimia.

According to the *Diagnostic and Statistical Manual of Mental Disorders* (DSM), which sets the standards for diagnosing mental disorders, in order for a diagnosis of anorexia, an individual must maintain a body weight less than 85 percent of that expected, and must not menstruate for three consecutive months, if the person is female.

A diagnosis of bulimia, according to the DSM, requires episodes of binge eating and purging—by vomiting, laxatives or other "compensatory" means—to occur at least twice a week for three months.

Whatever behaviors do not fit in either of those diagnoses are considered EDNOS, or Eating Disorder Not Otherwise Specified.

Being in the EDNOS category is a comfort to Sarah. It makes her "food issues" not that serious. But according to a 2009 study conducted by the University of Minnesota, it is. While considered a milder eating disorder, EDNOS has a higher mortality rate than both anorexia and bulimia.

For Rachel, meeting the DSM standards for anorexia is a badge of honor.

"I worked real hard for this, but I'm not there yet," she says wrapping her thumb and pointer finger around her left wrist. Rachel can touch all of her fingers to her thumb that way, but she wants her thumb to pass the nail bed of her pointer finger. "Before, I used to only be able to touch my middle finger and my ring finger to my thumb," she says, unable to hide her pride.

And she has the pictures to prove it—a photo gallery of her progress posted online. Underneath, the comments range from, "You are way too skinny, honey. Take care," to "I am so jealous."

Another comment is from a girl saying how bad she wants to be anorexic too. She asks Rachel, "How many calories do you eat per day?"

After that question, the gallery is locked, meaning no one can respond to the question, and the member is banned from posting on the site.

"You can usually tell when they are just here for tips and to learn how to be 'ana,'" says PJ, the 26-year-old woman who runs the website. "Then when you see they have only one or two posts, they're done."

Every time a member posts something, either a question or a reply, there is a ticker that keeps track of how many posts the person has made on that particular site. Most members have at least 1,000. Many have 20,000. The ones who have fewer than 100 have to prove they are there for the proper reasons, PJ says.

"We do not want people coming in here to learn how to make themselves sick," says PJ. "We have very strict rules. If you have an ED [eating disorder], then you are welcome here, we provide a community. But if you don't, if you just want to look good in your bikini, then goodbye. We don't want people like that here."

And many of those who end up on support sites are those with functional disorders, those who have hidden their behaviors so well in their everyday lives they don't feel they need treatment, or just don't want it. They seem to have everything else together, and PJ says this can give a false sense of security

Being Not Pro Is Cool

There is ... [a] big change on the net. . . . Being not pro is now cool. MiAna [referring to MiAna Land, a pro–eating disorder support website] was kind of shunned for not being pro back in the day . . . not anymore. Present-day MiAna has been a groundbreaker in the ED [eating disorder] site world. The things this place has done, and what it became has set a path all its own.

MiAna Land, "About MiAna Land," May 23, 2011. www.mianaland.com.

to many who know on some level they have a good chance of dying from their disorders, but somehow still feel it won't happen to them.

Friendly Fire

Ruth, an anorexic, is an emergency room doctor who sips 90 calories of chicken broth in between patients in order to keep her electrolytes level—and to keep from passing out. When she really gets hungry, she looks at "food porn" or pictures of food she wants to eat, but can't, by searching Google Images. And she's not the only doctor who frequents here.

Ruth's knowledge doesn't keep her from engaging in disordered behavior; it helps her perfect it.

"I know I should know better," she says. "I take precautions."

And she shares those precautions with other members of her online community.

"If there is a healthier, or less dangerous, way of—and I know this sounds bad—of starving yourself," she says, "I feel I have an obligation to tell them. It's no different than giving a clean needle to a drug addict; you do what's best in the moment, and some of these girls are very young and very naïve, and they will take chances that could end up killing them. That's when I step in."

And because so many members are successful students and professionals who are otherwise self-sufficient, those closest to them are often clueless. Many of the adults here have been hiding their disorders since their early teens.

"I go online after my husband falls asleep, and I always keep a second window open on the screen, so if he does wake up I just have to minimize what I don't want him to see," says Sarah.

In high school, when Sarah's eating disorder began, she says she would cut class and just eat all day.

"I would go drive through every fast-food joint in a 5-mile radius of my school and eat until I couldn't breathe," she says. "Then I would hate myself. And then I would go to this dumpster behind a CVS to get rid of all the wrappers before someone saw them."

Sarah says back then she would binge, but not purge by vomiting. She would fast for days after the binge in an effort to "purify" her body.

"Then I'd get so hungry I'd do it all over again," she says. "It became this vicious, shameful cycle, one that I was good at hiding."

Despite binging and purging once per day, Caitlyn, a pre-law student, doesn't believe she has a problem at all. "It's a bad habit. It's not a good thing, but neither is smoking."

After being a member of the site for four years and showing she was a responsible member, Caitlyn was chosen to be a moderator.

Moderators are like managers on the site. They censor discussions that give away dangerous tips. They break up arguments and arrange meet-ups for members. Three times a year hundreds of members from Caitlyn's site meet in California, New York and London. Some come from other countries to attend them.

"Does that sound crazy?" she asks. "These women are my family. They have helped me through some of the most difficult times of my life."

Caitlyn, 19, comes off as a completely together, confident and happy young woman. In one post she is helping another member with Calculus homework, in another she is talking a member through a breakup, and coaching another girl about why "dying young, thin and pretty" isn't actually better than dying "old and fat." But in another comment, Caitlyn sounds like a completely different person.

Posts like "How many calories will you burn giving blood?" "What did you binge on today?" or "What was your most embarrassing eating disorder moment?" are common around here and Caitlyn addresses the last one. She recalls sitting in a classroom next to her friend, who has no clue she has "food issues." Like Sarah, Caitlyn doesn't ever use the words "eating disorder."

"I don't like saying that," she says. "Maybe because I don't think I really have one sometimes."

Caitlyn says her friend was complaining about a smell in the room, when Caitlyn realized it was her.

She had dried vomit underneath her fingernails.

"Hey, things happen!" she jokingly says in the post.

There are more than 30 replies to "embarrassing eating disorder moments."

In another post Caitlyn worries about her teeth, after an older member says she has to have a bunch of her teeth pulled, even though she had only purged for a few months years ago. She says the dentist told her it was malnutrition that caused her teeth to rot and posts a picture of her teeth, a combination of yellow, brown and black stubs.

With holiday celebrations, games, contests and chat rooms included in the forum, and at least one hundred people available to speak to at any given time with only the click of a mouse, it is easy for relationships to form and personal information to be shared. And there are tight bonds here.

"Being here makes me feel less disgusting," says Andy, a 17-year-old girl who has been both anorexic and bulimic for the past three years. "There's this camaraderie that you form here, just by knowing you are not alone with your disorder." . . .

My Beloved Monster

Amy, 18, a former moderator on a support site with 300 members—not a pro-ana site, she says adamantly—spent three years in what she calls "a dangerous, well-intentioned sisterhood that at one time felt like it was saving my life, but also prolonged my disorder and normalized it."

She describes fights between members of different support sites and "mods" (short for "moderators") arguing because one site would accuse the other of posting "tips" or was considered "too soft and flaky" or was considered too harsh and mean. Because of this, she says, her site eventually began screening members and making them go through an application and interviewing process. New members had to be formally accepted.

Since she has left, the site no longer accepts new members at all. Many current members wear red bracelets made of string so they can identify each other if they ever meet in public.

Amy recalls one time where a member 3,000 miles away said she was going to kill herself and then signed off the website.

"What are you supposed to do in that situation? We aren't professionals and a lot of people who go to those boards sometimes need professional help."

Amy contacted the owner of the site, who then contacted a local police department who then contacted a police department in the member's country who then went to her home and found her alive and well.

"It's hard because everything seems good and normal, and then one day this happens and you have someone else's life in your hands and what do you do from the other side of a computer screen?"

Jessica, 25, has also left her support site after seven years. Jessica's site had about 600 members from around the world. She says she felt like it was impossible to get better in a place where she was surrounded by so many people who were worse, so she had to end a lot of her friendships.

"I've flown across the country to be in one girl's bridal party," she says. "The love I had and that I still have for these people is very real. But as the years passed, I realized I was creating my own reality, and creating this new kind of 'normal' that wasn't normal at all. My eating disorder wasn't something weird about me, it was what made me fit [in], and I withdrew more and more from reality and my life. I would be at family gatherings on holidays and sneaking on the computer, I needed the site to get me through my day and all of my fears about what I would have to eat."

Jessica describes a five-minute ritual she would perform every time she left the site, one of logging out, deleting cookies and history and auto completes from search engines, and the nightmares she would have of her parents finding out she was there.

"I think parents should be aware of what their kids are doing. I think the media needs to be aware of what it's doing," says Amy. "Because it was [a TV show] that introduced me to pro-ana sites, which then brought me to the support sites. It was a pretty actress, the glamour that drew me in at first. Not a sick girl. And then I found a place where I felt normal, when what I was doing wasn't normal. And if I didn't find that, if I didn't find other people like me, I don't think this would have gone as far as it did."

In her final days on the site, Amy says she saw a picture posted by one of the members of a bulimic girl vomiting after a binge.

She was dead.

Her stomach tore open from the repeated purging, her body was purple and swollen with the food that leaked out of her stomach.

Her head was still in the toilet.

On Both Sides

Back on Rachel's site, there are people looking for her, asking if anyone has heard from her. Rachel had lost Internet access for a few days and couldn't access the site.

One member writes that she is worried and wishes she could give all this up.

"It just makes me think 'cause my ED has wasted so much of my life but I can't stop," she says. "And even if I could push a button and make this all go away and be normal, I don't know that I would."

Under her profile picture she has written, "LW: 100 CW: 104 HW: 160 GW: 90," meaning her low weight was 100 lbs., her current weight is 104, her high weight was 160 and her goal weight is 90. Many other members have the same abbreviations under their pictures, with varying numbers.

When regulars go missing for even a few days, it is cause for alarm. Members have died before.

"Occasionally the worst happens, but most times it's because they get caught up in their everyday lives," says PJ. "Sometimes it's because they decide to recover."

Two of PJ's site members died of heart attacks brought on by their eating disorders in the past five years. "Would that have happened with or without my site? Probably," says PJ. "I want to say what I'm doing is helping because I do believe it is. I think we would hurt a lot more people by shutting down."

PJ recalls one member who was hospitalized for having low electrolytes in her blood from purging, a condition that can cause cardiac arrest, telling her, "If only my heart was outside of my body, I would put it in a container, and I would take such good care of it."

She says it's not that her members are unaware of the dangers of their behavior, it's that they can't stop. And, at least here, she can give them an outlet for their emotions, and people who will listen and relate to them without passing judgment.

PJ has no intention of closing her site anytime soon, and even Jessica, who says she will never rejoin the community again, is unsure whether these support sites are helping those with eating disorders or hurting them.

"I think it helped me when I needed it most, but if I were to go back it would only hurt me, not intentionally, because those people are some of the best people I have ever met in my life," says Jessica. "I'm not going to say being there is wrong or bad because I've been on both sides. And nothing is that black and white. I only know that it isn't the right thing for me right now. And if I could meet these friends I've had for so many years in another time or place, it would be different. I wish it could be different."

> "What seems most significant about the thinspiration videos is that they're not propaganda or even entertainment, but an effort, however misguided, at art."

Thinspiration Videos Are Misguided Attempts at Artistic Expression

Virginia Heffernan

Virginia Heffernan is a columnist for the New York Times *and covers digital technology and culture. In the following viewpoint, she claims that "thinspiration" videos, online clips with photos of waifish models and self-portraits of anorexic women, are personal and artistic. Though created to inspire weight loss, thinspiration videos appear to also deter eating disorders with morbid imagery, Heffernan claims. In fact, she regards them as multimedia journal entries that reuse and juxtapose existing material such as photography, film, and music to tell personal stories.*

As you read, consider the following questions:

1. How does Heffernan describe the photos of bodies in thinspiration videos?

2. Why is government intervention of thinspiration videos futile, in Heffernan's opinion?

3. In the author's view, what type of woman from the tradition of confessional poetry and diaries appear in thinspiration videos?

You don't have to search very hard to find the excruciating online videos known as thinspiration, or thinspo. Photomontages of skeletal women, including some celebrities and models, play all over the Internet, uploaded from the United States, Germany, Holland and elsewhere. These videos are designed to "inspire" viewers—to fortify their ambitions. But exactly which ambitions? To lose weight, presumably. To stop losing weight, possibly. Thinspo videos profess a range of ideologies, often pressing morbid images into double service, as both goads and deterrents to anorexia.

Thinspiration videos are a cryptic art with rigid rules, as much a formula as a form. As listless, pounding or archly chipper music plays, still photos of one wraith after another surface and fade. The women are generally solitary and sullen, or entirely faceless. Bony self-portraits, created in bathroom mirrors by anonymous photographers, have faces that have been obscured or cropped out. Many figures in the videos are supine, as in the pervasive hipbone self-portrait, which seems to be shot by a photographer on her back aiming a camera at her abdomen and the waistband of her jeans. A bird's-eye shot of the thighless legs of a seated figure is also common. The soundtracks to thinspiration videos, some of which feature songs explicitly about starvation, are not subtle. *Skeleton, you are my friend. I will sacrifice all I have in life. Bones are beautiful. Hey, baby, can you bleed like me?*

Filmmakers are reticent with commentary. If they explain their images in any way, it's with oddly peppy title cards ("Enjoy!" "Thanks for watching!") or a series of unsigned quotations, compiled as if for a commonplace book. A thinspiration auteur makes her voice heard almost exclusively through these cards, and she sometimes uses them to plead with her audience to go easy on her work or to stay tuned for further thinspo. I've never seen a thinspo video with a voice-over or even moving images.

Shooting photos just for a video is also rare. Instead, thinspiration consists of personal, archival and file photos (some taken from Photobucket and other photo-sharing sites) that have been inventively sequenced and edited, often using the so-called Ken Burns effect of pressing in on significant details. Focusing on shadows around the pelvises, ribs, knees and spines of underweight women, the most extreme thinspiration filmmakers eschew not just muscle and fat but seemingly all human tissue. The ghastly subgenre known as "bones thinspo" shows some bodies that must surely be corpses.

Agony and Lightness

Like ballet and some forms of modern dance, thinspiration puts a premium on both agony and lightness. It also carries a fierce ethic of self-sacrifice. "Sacrifice," many of the title cards instruct, "is giving up something good for something better." A video by the prolific Chewing Cotton Productions flashes this quotation: "Time spent wasting is not wasted time." There is also haunting poetry about a desire to be exempted from natural laws, including this passage, which appears with variations in several of the videos: "I want to be so thin, light, airy that, when the light hits me, I don't leave a shadow behind. When I walk across the snow I will not leave so much as one footprint to mar its virgin purity. I can dance between the raindrops in a downpour."

What should we make of this provocative, even chilling material? Like other kinds of photography involving young women, thinspiration is regarded by some as a moral outrage, even a public health threat. (This response is much rarer when subjects and consumers of a form are men—as with pro-bodybuilding "bigspiration" videos.) Last month [April 2008], the lower house of the French Parliament proposed outlawing any online incitement to anorexia, including thinspiration videos and some 400 Web sites that seem to advocate anorexia and bulimia with words and pictures. The bill's sponsor, a lawmaker named Valérie Boyer, argued that "the sociocultural and media environment seems to favor the emergence of troubled nutritional behavior."

From the looks of the thinspo images, "troubled nutritional behavior" seems like an understatement. Many of those who post comments about the videos are as horrified by them as Boyer is, and the debate over pro-anorexia material is nowhere more heated than in the YouTube comments section. "You are not only killing yourself but you are killing other girls as well," wrote someone called artslave411 on a recent thinspiration video. Someone shot back: "As if some pictures could make you become an anorexic. . . . All I want to say: Don't think of pictures as that powerful!"

Government intervention in this debate seems futile. Leaving aside the fantasy of ever controlling the cultural climate—a force of nature that is no longer incorporated only in production studios, publishing companies, radio stations and television outlets—it's not entirely clear that thinspiration should be considered "media" rather than a highly idiosyncratic response to it. This material presents itself as subversive and defiant, and thinspo collections are much closer to multimedia journal entries than they are to TV shows or fashion spreads in glossy magazines. What's more, many thinspo sites make explicit their opposition to popular culture, approvingly offering images of women deemed "too skinny by media standards."

Traditional and Digital

On a formal level, thinspiration rejects the conventions of propaganda and advertising, instead borrowing devices from two other forms, one traditional and one digital. The traditional form is women's confessional poems and diaries, including the work of Sylvia Plath, Anne Sexton and Louise Glück. A woman who is furtive, prolific, deeply melancholy, proud of her sacrifices, furious at her family's various offenses, frustrated with her body and protective of her supreme right to destroy herself—this persona, in America, at least, was the invention of poets like Plath, whose teasing and savage voice, even now, is every bit as bracing as the thinspo videos. The cacophony of female archetypes in Plath's work—little girl ("Daddy, daddy"), avenging Cassandra ("Do I terrify?") and wan martyr ("the long gone darlings")—turn up in the thinspiration videos, too, which feature women looking alternately like schoolgirls, madwomen and saints. Sarcasm and assonance characterize thinspo poetry: "Eat no evil."

The second influence, from digital culture, is the so-called recuts: videos that take existing photography and film and use music and new juxtapositions to create a story that's at odds with a master narrative. (An example: the fictional trailers that tease out a gay, *Brokeback Mountain* plot from virtually every mainstream blockbuster.) Film of runway shows, as it appears on fashion Web sites, presents the models as confident, beautiful, "fierce," where the same roll, in the hands of a thinspo filmmaker, can make them look disfigured and diseased.

Setting aside the mystifying proposition that anorexia be seen as a lifestyle choice (as some extremist pro-anorexia sites maintain), as well as the age-old riddle of whether popular culture can produce mental illness, what seems most significant about the thinspiration videos is that they're not propaganda or even entertainment, but an effort, however misguided, at art. One thinspiration filmmaker whose YouTube screen name is "hungryhell," and who spoke on condition of anonymity to keep her struggles with bulimia private from people who know her, emphasized to me in an e-mail message that her work "represents what I have been feeling at that time in particular." She added, "The songs I use . . . say exactly what I need to but can't figure out how."

Hungryhell's films are intricate, many of them augmenting the thinspo formula with collage, typography, still lifes, art photography and even painting. I asked her how she does it. "Putting it together is not hard," she wrote back, explaining that she uses Windows Movie Maker software. "When I am feeling something, it just all comes together."

"These sites have harmful effects on users as they intensify weight/shape concerns and negative affect, and introduce users to new methods of weight loss."

Pro-Ana Websites Should Be Regulated

Royal College of Psychiatrists

The Royal College of Psychiatrists is the professional and educational body for psychiatrists in the United Kingdom. In the following viewpoint, the Royal College of Psychiatrists states that sites promoting anorexia ("pro-ana") and bulimia ("pro-mia") should be regulated. It supports efforts to encourage the Internet industry to develop voluntary practices that protect child safety and raise parental awareness of pro–eating disorder groups on the Internet. Instead of making pro-ana and pro-mia sites illegal, services should be provided to their visitors and online discussions of harmful eating behaviors should be moderated, recommends the Royal College of Psychiatrists.

As you read, consider the following questions:

1. How should pro-eating disorders sites be addressed in schools, according to the Royal College of Psychiatrists?

2. What does the Royal College of Psychiatrists call for the media to do?

3. What is worrying about pro-recovery websites, according to the Royal College of Psychiatrists?

The eating disorders, anorexia nervosa, bulimia nervosa and related disorders, are biologically based serious mental disorders with high levels of mortality, physical and psychological morbidity and disability and impaired quality of life. Cognitive and emotional functioning are impaired and this may make engagement in treatment difficult. These disorders have a peak age of onset in adolescence, at a time in life when peer influences are particularly strong. Social contagion effects in the onset and maintenance of eating disorders have been noted, such as the clustering of eating disordered attitudes and behaviours in peer/friendship groups of young people and also within wider social units (schools) or geographical units.

What Are Pro-Anorexia Websites and What Is Their Effect?

Pro-anorexia ('pro-ana') and pro-bulimia ('pro-mia') websites advocate anorexia nervosa or bulimia nervosa as a lifestyle choice rather than as serious mental disorders, and typically contain tips and tricks on how to maintain or initiate new anorexic/bulimic behaviours and how to resist treatment or recovery. The most frequent motivation cited by users of these sites is to maintain motivation to lose weight, to get personal support and to meet other people with eating disorders.

Such websites have been in existence since the development of the Internet, but have grown significantly in recent years and are now available on social networking sites like Facebook. The limited research available has shown that a significant number of teenage girls visit these sites, in particular those at high risk of eating disorders. A substantial proportion of young people who already have an eating disorder also visit them, in particular those with a more severe form of the illness. Nearly all report learning new weight loss techniques from these sites. Worryingly, young people with eating disorders also report learning new weight loss techniques from pro-recovery websites (i.e., those set up by people who have overcome an eating disorder), although to a much lesser extent than from pro-eating disorders sites. Parents of eating disorder sufferers have a limited awareness of pro-anorexia sites and of their child's use of such sites.

What Attempts Have Been Made to Deal with These Sites?

In the UK and USA a number of position statements from reputable organizations for patients, carers and professionals in the eating disorders field have expressed concerns about the effect of these sites on vulnerable young people (Beat [Beating Eating Disorders], AED [Academy for Eating Disorders], NEDA [National Eating Disorders Association], ANAD [National Association of Anorexia Nervosa and Associated Disorders]).

In the UK an Early Day Motion was tabled in Feb 2008 by a LibDem [Liberal Democrat] member of Parliament calling on the government '*to investigate ways to deal with such sites, which cause devastation for people and families, and to support sites which offer help and advice to victims and parents.*'

In March 2008 the [psychologist Tanya] Byron review on 'Safer Children in a Digital World' was published by the Department for Children, Schools and Families and the Department for Culture, Media and Sport. The review proposed the development of '*national strategy for child Internet safety which involves better self-regulation and better provision of information and education for children and families.'* The conclusions from this review were fully accepted by the House of Commons Culture, Media and Sport Committee which in July 2008, published a report on 'Harmful content on the Internet and in video games.' In Sept. 2008, a UK Council for Child Internet Safety was launched by the government. One of its key tasks will be to develop a Strategy for Child Internet Safety. A detailed action plan with milestones, based on the Byron review has also been published, detailing how the newly established council in collaboration with the industry and other partners will develop an independently monitored voluntary code of practice for the Internet industry, will raise awareness of e-safety amongst parents, children and others, and will support schools to deliver on e-safety. These initiatives do not specifically refer to pro-eating disorders websites, but their content is highly relevant in this context.

Legislators in other countries have also been concerned. In France, there were attempts to make pro-eating disorders sites illegal in 2008, but the bill was ultimately not passed. In the Netherlands, the Minister for Youth and Families called for 'click-through warnings' to be added to all pro-anorexia sites hosted on Dutch Internet services earlier this year.

The responses of Internet and social networking site providers to questions and complaints about such sites have been varied, ranging from reluctance to censor or ban such sites to deleting them or inserting banner adverts into these sites, advertising pro-recovery organizations.

Summary and Call for Action

There is growing evidence that pro-eating disorder websites attract vulnerable young people at risk from eating disorders and also those with eating disorders. These sites have harmful effects on users as they intensify weight/shape concerns and

Three Main Concerns

There has been extensive debate about whether pro-ana [pro-anorexia] sites should be allowed to operate. Those wanting the sites banned have three main concerns:

- Vulnerable people will visit the sites and be exposed to information and attitudes that will trigger or worsen their eating disorders.

- Pro-ana sites foster undesirable competition and unhealthy weight loss habits.

- The sites promote anorexia by portraying it as a valid lifestyle choice and even as a virtue akin to a religious quest.

Christine Halse, Anne Honey, and Desiree Boughtwood, Inside Anorexia: The Experiences of Girls and Their Families. *Philadelphia, PA: Jessica Kingsley Publishers, 2008.*

negative affect, and introduce users to new methods of weight loss. Parents usually have little awareness of these sites.

In view of this, we make the following recommendations:

1. We applaud the government's efforts to increase child Internet safety via the newly launched UK Council for Child Internet Safety, and through industry self-regulation, an integrated child e-safety strategy and a clear action plan. These plans should include pro-eating disorder sites in their discussions of harmful web content.

2. Pro-eating disorder websites are likely to be set up and maintained by young people who themselves have an eating disorder. In view of this, making them illegal

would lead to criminalising a vulnerable group of young people. The Byron action plan mentions '*joint working between industry and the third sector to improve the support offered to vulnerable groups, including providing links to support services and improving moderation practices where users discuss harmful behaviours.*' These measures should be extended to explicitly include pro-eating disorders websites.

3. Likewise, the measures proposed in the Byron action plan to raise awareness of e-safety amongst parents and teachers should specifically address pro-eating disorder sites and their harmful effects. Such educational efforts need to be coordinated with wider efforts to educate parents and teachers in the early detection and management of eating disorder symptoms.

4. We call upon the media not to make pro-ana websites into headline news, not to report their content in a sensationalised way and not to report how to access them, as this may lead to increased use of such sites. Guidance for the media on reporting of pro-ana sites should be part of the development of wider guidance to them on de-sensationalising reporting on eating disorders in general. There are clear parallels here to the area of suicide prevention where it has been shown that the way in which suicides are reported can [increase] or decrease suicide rates.

5. We acknowledge that eating disorders often leave sufferers feel[ing] isolated, ashamed and cut off from support and that online support is an easily accessible and powerful way of providing support to those people. We encourage young people with eating disorders and their families to use reputable sources of information and support such as that provided by Beat.

> *"Wouldn't we [be] better off engaging these pro-ana people and websites directly?"*

Pro-Ana Websites Should Not Be Regulated

Adam Thierer

In the following viewpoint, Adam Thierer contends that sites that advocate or glorify anorexia ("pro-ana") should not be banned or subjected to regulations. The author insists that efforts should engage pro-ana individuals and groups in discussions about their encouragement of dangerous lifestyles. Banning or regulating pro-ana sites, he alleges, would force them underground and drive eating disorders from the view of experts and families. Thierer is president of the Progress & Freedom Foundation (PFF) and director of its Center for Digital Media Freedom (CDMF).

As you read, consider the following questions:

1. How did the French bill propose to punish pro-ana sites, as stated in the viewpoint?

2. If the government can regulate sites that glorify "excessive thinness," what else can it do, in Thierer's opinion?

Adam Thierer, "Can the French Really Ban Pro-Thin Websites?," *Tech Liberation Front*, April 16, 2008. Reproduced by permission of the author.

3. What is the positive side of pro-ana sites, as suggested by the author?

There are a lot of disturbing things out there on the Internet. I don't think I need to provide an inventory. Occasionally, some of the more despicable sites (think pro-suicide sites or bomb-making sites) capture the attention of public policy makers and bans are proposed. It was only a matter of time, therefore, before "pro-ana" [pro-anorexia] sites made the regulatory radar screen as they did this week [in April 2008] when lawmakers in France proposed a measure, "aimed at fighting incitement to extreme thinness or anorexia."

The pro-ana movement, which refers to people and websites that justify or glorify anorexia or an excessively "thin look" or lifestyle, came to my attention last year when an academic was interviewing me for a new book he was writing about online responsibility. He was asking me what I thought about the idea of liability being imposed on website developers who glorify potentially harmful lifestyles or activities. In other words, an "aiding and abetting" standard for hateful or "harmful" online speech. I expected our discussion to focus on the truly sick or stupid stuff out there—like the bomb-recipe nutjobs or the suicide fans—but, instead, the academic mentioned pro-ana sites. . . . The danger of these sites is that they offer young girls, which seems to be the primary audience, very unhealthy advice about how they can use various techniques (fasting, vomiting, laxatives, etc.) to become super-thin. Needless to say, that can lead to extreme weight loss and serious health disorders for these girls.

The French Law

Should sites be banned, or held liable in some fashion, for the harm they cause? We could nitpick about whether or not pro-ana sites cause serious harm to girls, but let's assume that they do cause *some* harm. Does that mean the site administrators should be held responsible for the actions of others who read those sites? The French law says "yes." It would, according, to Reuters:

> impose penalties of two years plus a fine of 30,000 euros ($47,450) for "incitement to excessive thinness by publicizing of any kind." The penalties would rise to three years in jail plus a 45,000 euros fine in cases where a death was caused by anorexia. The bill was adopted by the lower house of Parliament on Tuesday and must go before the Senate before it becomes law. [Editor's note: It was not approved by the Senate.]

One response to such a measure will be that it will encounter significant enforcement challenges. Ironically, we've been here before; at least the French have. You will recall the famous Yahoo! case regarding the sale or bartering of Nazi paraphernalia online. . . .

But I don't want to talk about enforcement challenges or extraterritorial jurisdictional issues here, even though I think they are significant. Nor do I want to dwell on the free speech issues at hand, which are also numerous. Just to name one: If government can regulate sites that glorify "excessive thinness," what about sites that potentially encourage the opposite by "glorifying" the consumption of fatty foods or sweets? Should *Crispy on the Outside*, which is produced by our own Jerry Brito, qualify for regulation or liability if someone gets excessive cholesterol-clogged arteries after eating too much of what that site recommends? Jerry . . . perhaps you need to get a lawyer!

Or what about a website that featured a mix of pro-ana and anti-ana viewpoints but that still contained a lot of the same "harmful" information that the strictly pro-ana sites featured. Should it be banned? I could go on all day with similar examples.

Don't Drive Them Underground

But what I instead want to focus on here is this: Wouldn't we [be] better off engaging these pro-ana people and websites directly? That is, don't ban them or drive them underground, but instead go directly to those sites ourselves and engage in a discussion about what most of us would regard as unhealthy lifestyles.

It certainly may be true that pro-ana sites encourage unhealthy, even harmful, lifestyles. But the problem is right there; it is out in the open for us to see and address through discussion, education, and opposing websites. As I have pointed out in my work on social networking sites, we may not like some of the things that others (especially youngsters) post online, but the one significant upside of it is that it highlights problems that used to be well out of our view. Indeed, in past generations, parents often warned their kids to behave themselves in public or else "it will go down on your permanent record." It was largely just a scare tactic, because there really was no "permanent record" of the mundane activities of youth. Today, however—for better or for worse—the Internet is becoming "your permanent record." No doubt, this raises some serious, long-term privacy concerns. But the one positive aspect of this is that it makes it easier for us to identify and address certain problems.

From what I have heard about pro-ana sites, all this is already happening to a limited degree. Apparently, some parents and even health professionals are intervening on these sites and trying to provide balanced viewpoints or warning girls of the potential downsides. And other sites have developed to counter and address the pro-ana movement. Moreover, part of the health education curricula in school can include discussions of eating disorders. Currently, most of the discussion has been about the opposite problem: obesity and a sedentary lifestyle. What we need to focus on, of course, is moderation and healthy lifestyle choices.

Education and open, informed discussion is the best answer here. I fear that by trying to regulate these sites, we simply drive the problem—and the discussion—underground.

Periodical and Internet Sources Bibliography

The following articles have been selected to supplement the diverse views presented in this chapter.

Siri Agrell	"The Perils of Legislating a Health Aesthetic," *Globe and Mail*, April 19, 2008.
Katie J.M. Baker	"Body-Positive Blogs: Helpful or Hurtful?," *Refinery 29*, June 30, 2011.
Jenifer Goodwin	"Pro-Eating Disorder Sites Abound on the Internet," *Bloomberg BusinessWeek*, June 17, 2010.
Jacqueline Head	"Seeking 'Thinspiration,'" BBC News, August 8, 2007.
Carly Levy	"Those Perilous Pro-Anorexia Websites," Pale Reflections, November 21, 2007. www.pale-reflections.com.
David Ma	"Smoke and Mirrors—Pro-Anorexia Websites Normalize Eating Disorders, Put Patients at Risk," *AAP News*, April 2009.
Tina Peng	"Out of the Shadows," *Newsweek*, November 22, 2008.
Amanda Schoenberg	"Biting Back: As Pro-Eating Disorder Web Sites Emerge, So Does the Backlash," *Albuquerque Journal*, March 9, 2009.
Justin Thomas	"Sick Support: How Websites Encourage Bulimia, Anorexia's Ugly Sister," *National*, July 25, 2010.
Anthony Van Pham	"Inside Toronto's Secret Pro-Anorexia Community," The Dashing Fellows, January 13, 2009. www.thedashingfellows.com.

OPPOSING
VIEWPOINTS®
SERIES

CHAPTER 4

How Should Eating Disorders Be Treated?

Chapter Preface

In the Maudsley, or family-based, approach to treating anorexia nervosa in adolescents, parents "re-feed" their child to a healthy weight with a therapist's guidance. It requires close monitoring of nutrition and meals, which can escalate to standoffs at the dining table. Christina Grieco of Chantilly, Virginia, credits the Maudsley approach with her recovery from anorexia. "I think the only way that eating disorders should be treated is to take the control away from the eating disorder so that it becomes powerless," she says in the February 24, 2009, *Washington Post*, "and give control to the parents who can make sound decisions for their child and make them nourished again."

This aspect of the Maudsley approach is misperceived as force-feeding, according to advocates. "If anyone tells you that the Maudsley approach consists of 'holding down your daughter and forcing food into her mouth,' they are wrong," maintains Angela Celio Doyle, a clinical psychologist in the University of Chicago's eating disorders program. "The treatment involves compassionate, yet persistent and firm expectations that your adolescent eat an amount of food that can reverse the state of starvation his or her body is in and help them gain weight." Doyle also insists that it "is not punitive in any way and involves quite a bit of emotional support."

However, others contend that Maudsley does involve force-feeding. "It has to, because most anorexics are not able to eat unless they are given no other alternative," argues psychologist Sarah Ravin. "Call it whatever you want—supported nutrition, letting them eat, helping them recover, empowering parents to combat eating disorder symptoms—all of these labels are quite accurate and descriptive. So is force-feeding. And I don't believe it is a bad thing," she states.

In the following chapter, the authors discuss the numerous treatments available for eating disorders.

> *"Detention of patients with severe anorexia nervosa is ethically justified, may be necessary, and should be covered by legislation."*

Involuntary Treatment for Anorexia Is Justified

Cornelia Thiels

In the following viewpoint, Cornelia Thiels affirms that involuntary treatment of patients with anorexia is justified in life-threatening circumstances. She claims that full recovery is of greater value than autonomy, which is already diminished by the disease. Involuntary treatment does not always imply force-feeding or tube feeding, the author maintains, and highly skilled nursing and patient admission before her body mass index drops to a critical threshold is preferred. Thiels is a psychiatric physician and professor of socialized medicine at Bielefeld University of Applied Sciences in Germany.

As you read, consider the following questions:

1. As described by Thiels, what is not included in the criteria of capacity?

Cornelia Thiels, "Forced Treatment of Patients with Anorexia," *Current Opinion in Psychiatry*, vol. 21, September 2008, pp. 495–498. All rights reserved. Reproduced by permission.

2. What are the legal procedures and ethics in the United States in regard to involuntary treatment, as claimed by Thiels?

3. How should coercion be used in feeding, as advised in the viewpoint?

The mortality associated with anorexia nervosa is high and respecting patient autonomy may have a fatal outcome. Some fully recovered patients are grateful for the compassionate care they have received, which they had previously regarded as coercive. A database search of Medline, PsycINFO, PsycARTICLES, and Social Sciences Citation Index with the key words anorexia nervosa combined with forced treatment, compulsory treatment, mental capacity, mental health act, mental health section, and mental health law from 1984 up to 25 January 2008 identified one paper published in 2007 and three in 2006. Two articles in German will be summarized in detail for those unable to read the original.

Complexity of an Interdisciplinary and International Debate

Among others, physicians, lawyers, philosophers, psychologists, patients and their parents, members of departments of management and of dietetics have contributed in the absence of an agreed terminology. There is agreement that child and adult patients need to be treated differently for both legal and developmental reasons. The legal situation differs between and even within countries. Common and statutory law, guardianship and mental health acts all play a role.

Definitions

'Capacity' (in the USA 'competence') is the legal term for the ability to make treatment choices. It requires, first, the ability to understand and retain treatment information about the illness and its consequences, the treatments and their benefits and risks and to believe this information; second, the ability to weigh up this information for decision making; and third, the ability to make a free choice. These criteria do not include attitudes and values, personality and sense of identity, or ambivalence towards treatment and recovery, all of which are relevant in anorexia nervosa. Nor does the concept of capacity capture the suffering of patients with anorexia nervosa who struggle to be in control of themselves, an essential aspect of their psychopathology. Law—unlike psychiatry—generally intends to distinguish between the legal and the illegal and does not adapt quickly to the growth and change in clinical knowledge.

'Competence' is a clinical term similar to 'capacity' but may include additional aspects such as the influence of emotional states or mental illness, for example, on the ability to make consistent decisions over time.

'Compulsory treatment' does not imply forced or tube feeding, nor the use of an intravenous drip. The term may refer to detention only, not necessarily by restraint or on a locked ward.

'Informal' or 'voluntary' treatment of patients with anorexia nervosa may and often does include restriction of movement, exercise, and an obligation to finish meals—regarded by some authors as ethically problematic, especially if consent to such treatment has not been given freely.

Treatment 'resistance' can be distinguished from treatment 'refusal'; the latter may be considered 'an outright categorical resistance'.

'Mental illness' is defined in the legislation of some countries—such as Israel—by the presence of psychotic features. Anorexia nervosa does not meet this criterion. In the Australian state of Victoria, anorexia nervosa fits the legal definition of mental illness as a 'medical condition of thought, mood, perception or memory'. The 1990 Mental Health Act of New

South Wales (NSW) covers anorexia nervosa, as it impairs 'mental functioning' and is accompanied by 'sustained or repeated irrational behaviour'.

'Guardian' is defined by the *Encyclopaedia Britannica* as a 'person legally entrusted with supervision of another who is ineligible to manage his own affairs'. Legal guardianship, available in some countries, is perceived as less stigmatizing than mental health legislation; it has the disadvantage, however, of lacking the controls necessary in compulsory hospitalization.

Empirical Research

[Researchers A.] Thiel and [T.] Paul review the sparse empirical research on compulsory treatment of anorexia nervosa— four studies from Australia, England, the USA and Germany published between 1997 and 2006. All are retrospective case note studies that report clinically significant increases in BMI [body mass index] of 3–4 kg/m^2. A 1-year follow-up interview was planned for the 15 Australian patients; however, one had died and only three participated. In a study carried out in London, the mortality rate in 81 detained patients was significantly higher (12 versus 2.5%) than an equal number of voluntary patients after a mean of 5.7 years. The detained patients, however, had been hospitalized more often before the index admission and reported more childhood sexual and physical abuse as well as self-harm. Thus, the less favourable long-term outcome is probably due to a more intractable illness in conjunction with personality problems rather than due to the detention itself. No follow-up is reported for the two other samples.

Forced Treatment in One German Unit

Twenty-five female patients aged 16–39 were admitted 'with severely life-threatening anorexia nervosa' and 'no motivation for treatment' (all translations by the author). Five agreed to inpatient treatment. Guardianship had been arranged before admission for seven patients—for six of them this was initiated by doctors who were not from the study hospital; for one, by the family. In all cases the court identified that the reason for guardianship was the patients' inability, due to illness, to take responsibility for their own affairs or their health. The decision to arrange guardianship was made for several reasons: the wish to end treatment immediately and be discharged; several years of unsuccessful therapy; inability to communicate about treatment; and 'massively manipulative behaviour and active prevention of feeding'. Only seven of 18 patients were persuaded by their guardian to accept informal inpatient treatment. The other 11 patients did not agree to treatment in a locked ward or to the elements of the treatment deemed necessary, and insisted on immediate discharge. Two of three legal minors were admitted involuntarily based on family law. Forced treatment lasted 6–27 weeks and ended before discharge in 11 of 13 cases, as these patients agreed to informal treatment. The remaining two patients agreed to transfer to a psychosomatic hospital after the end of involuntary admission in the study hospital.

Immediately after admission, those in an acutely life-threatening state were transferred to the ICU [intensive care unit]. Nineteen patients were treated with antidepressants for 'mild to medium severe depressive syndromes'. A treatment contract was individually worded for each patient, and it included weight gain of 0.7–1.0 kg per week. If their state of health allowed, patients were first given the opportunity to try to gain weight in a locked ward by eating independently or consuming high-calorie fluids. The time allowed for this approach was not stated; motivational interviewing, nursing or persuasion to eat are not mentioned. If patients failed to gain weight a feeding tube was inserted with their own or their guardians' agreement. This was the case in 22 out of 25 cases; in 20 patients, a PEG (transdermal duodenal tube) was used, four of these being informal patients. One patient was repeatedly isolated and physically restrained and gained only 1.11 kg in 178 days.

The aim to 'motivate' patients after re-feeding to accept further inpatient therapy was not achieved in all cases. Only 15 of 25 were transferred to a 'psychiatric-psychosomatic hospital', one to a psychiatric hospital, one to a unit of child and adolescent psychiatry, and five to a 'psychotherapeutic shared flat with an emphasis on the treatment of eating disorders'. Three wanted and found outpatient therapy for themselves.

'At the beginning of therapy, the patients often showed massive resistance'. One said: 'So far I have beaten everybody and have not put on weight. Here too, I will win'. Some patients 'manipulated' their PEG. This paper suggests the presence of counter-transference problems and battles rather than cooperation between patients and staff. The authors recommend continued guardianship for around 2 years to allow early intervention in the event of a relapse. So far, no follow-up has been published.

In patients with anorexia nervosa compulsorily detained in London, 'skilled nursing staff to establish a psychotherapeutic milieu and persuade the patients to eat substantial meals of gradually increasing caloric content over the course of admission' was shown to lead to sufficient weight gain without forced or tube feeding. It could be argued that this 'lenient' treatment was possible in London because the BMI at admission was 14.2 (SD 7.3) kg/m^2 whereas in Munich it was only 12.09 (SD 1.51) kg/m^2. If this was the case it suggests the need for earlier compulsory admission in order to avoid forced feeding. In Germany, unlike the UK, however, most nurses are not university educated and are less respected than their colleagues in British hospitals where hierarchy is less in evidence.

Factors Influencing Who Will Receive Forced Treatment

A retrospective study of the records of an Australian anorexia programme compares informal and compulsory admissions in 75 patients. Of 96 hospitalizations, 27 'were under mental health committal or adult guardianship orders'. Seven admissions were informal after '"strategic" initiation and abandonment of resort to law'. Thirty-six per cent were under the age of 20 years. The mean duration of hospitalization was 49 days and 40% of admissions lasted less than 3 weeks. The number of previous inpatient treatments was significantly higher for the coerced group, as was the number of psychiatric comorbidities, while the admission BMI was lower (13.2, SD 1.67 kg/m² versus 14.03, SD 1.84 kg/m²). In the coerced group a significantly higher proportion of patients were diagnosed with the potentially fatal re-feeding syndrome (10/16 versus 12/58), were kept in a locked ward (11/15 versus 1/69), and tube feeding was attempted for more of them (12/14 versus 11/59). The use of a locked ward and tube feeding were regarded as 'precursors' rather than 'by-products' of obtaining coercive orders. The powers of the Mental Health Act were used in the study unit to preserve physical integrity and safety of patients rather than to achieve an acceptable BMI or other treatment goals. Adult guardianship had 'usually' been tried before resorting to mental health committal.

Opinions

One German paper published in 1986 argues that readiness for treatment cannot be expected from patients with anorexia nervosa because of their physical and mental symptoms, as their thinking is distorted by body image disturbance and fear of gaining weight. [Researcher J.] Tiller et al. distinguished between the 'psychiatric symptom of a desire to avoid treatment leading to weight gain' and 'a decision to refuse medical intervention'. Tiller et al. do not accept 'that a patient with anorexia nervosa who does not wish to have treatment is comparable to a patient who refuses haemodialysis, as treatment prolongs life but is not curative', for 'many patients with anorexia nervosa make a complete recovery'. Thiel and Paul conclude that patients are entitled to forced treatment and that ethical judgement concerns not only actions but also failure to act. In contrast, a Polish psychologist has asked why drinking or overeating oneself to death is not prevented by compulsory detention while at least some of those with life-threatening anorexia nervosa receive forced treatment.

Legal Procedures and Ethics

If courts make the decision about involuntary treatment, as is the case in the USA, this procedure is utilized less frequently than if physicians make the initial admission subject to mental health tribunal review, as in Britain. The amount of risk/harm to self or others also plays a role. In the USA, for instance, because of the value placed on individual liberty, a high level of 'risk' has to be demonstrated. Using the law to persuade patients to accept informal treatment is ethically problematic.

In Germany, the constitution protects the two rights of freedom as well as the right not to be physically harmed. In cases of direct and imminent danger for the patient's life, detention and involuntary treatment are permitted by public law of the federal states or by using civil law guardianship. In 2004, the doctors treating a patient with anorexia nervosa were fined for accepting her refusal of any kind of feeding or intravenous drip. She was found in a coma and did not regain consciousness after treatment. The court argued that guardianship would have been granted for forced feeding had the doctors applied.

Recommendations

Among other recommendations made by Thiel and Paul are the following.

1. Coercion should not be used instead of psychotherapy nor does the former preclude the latter.

2. Applications should be made for guardianship for health and the possibility of detention for 3–6 months.

3. As mortality increases when weight decreases below a BMI of $13kg/m^2$, this is the suggested threshold for considering forced treatment. Suicidality, electrolyte imbalance, cardiac arrhythmia, and other acute mental or physical problems may also necessitate forced treatment.

4. Use coercion carefully and for the shortest time necessary. The interpersonal relationship and the psychotherapeutic milieu are more relevant for the course of treatment than is force.

5. As little coercion as possible should be used to ensure feeding. From the beginning patients should be motivated to eat with increasing independence.

6. Feeding and weight should not be unduly emphasized.

7. Treat with respect. Protect the dignity and fragile self-esteem of the anorexic patient.

8. Consider involving the family.

9. The aim is not a particular weight but the continuation of treatment without coercion.

The life of someone who may fully recover is of higher value than autonomy as this has already been compromised by anorexia nervosa. Thus, detention of patients with severe anorexia nervosa is ethically justified, may be necessary, and should be covered by legislation. Once the patient has been admitted to an eating disorder unit it is desirable and will usually be possible for improvement to be achieved with skilled nursing without the need to have recourse to forced or tube feeding. A multicentre register of particularly severe cases for the prospective recording of treatment and follow-up is urgently needed, as well as empirical research as a basis for a clinically useful re-definition of the terms 'competence' and 'capacity' in anorexia nervosa.

"*While generally treatment of anorexia results in improvement, these results are debatable for sufferers of extreme, chronic anorexia.*"

Involuntary Treatment for Anorexia May Not Be Justified in Some Cases

Avis Rumney

A former anorexic, Avis Rumney is an eating disorders specialist and author of Dying to Please: Anorexia, Treatment and Recovery. *In the following viewpoint, excerpted from* Dying to Please, *Rumney contends that involuntary treatment may cause more harm than good in severe cases of anorexia. She questions whether it is humane to intervene when the physically deteriorated patient has no chance of recovering to a normal life. Also, Rumney points out that often patients tear out legally authorized feeding tubes and that the benefits of aggressive feeding efforts will be temporary and likely to fail if encountered by resistance.*

Avis Rumney, *Dying to Please: Anorexia, Treatment and Recovery*. Jefferson, NC: McFarland & Company Inc., 2009, pp. 161–163. Copyright © McFarland & Company, 2009. All rights reserved. Reproduced by permission of McFarland & Company, Inc., Box 611, Jefferson NC 28640. www.mcfarlandpub.com.

As you read, consider the following questions:

1. What four elements determine the anorexic patient's right to refuse treatment, as described by the author?

2. In what situation can treatment in a hospital or outpatient setting create more harm than good, as stated by Rumney?

3. According to Rumney, what are the criteria indicating that a patient is not competent to make decisions on her own behalf?

Sometimes anorexics who are clearly in dire need of treatment refuse to seek help. When that anorexic is a minor, it is the responsibility of the parents or guardians to seek and provide treatment for her. If the anorexic who is a minor is in a hospital and still refuses treatment, then the parents in coordination with the staff have to choose the best route to assure the child's safety. However, an adult generally does not fall under the legal jurisdiction of her parents or anyone else, and the anorexic adult is entitled by law to refuse treatment. But there are situations in which the anorexic is undoubtedly psychologically and cognitively compromised and may be incapable of making a well-reasoned decision. She may appear quite lucid in all areas, except in evaluating her own condition, and she may be able to convince family and friends of her well-being despite her appearance. Family and friends may then assume her condition is not severe enough to warrant intervening, while in fact the anorexic's competence to choose or not choose treatment is impaired. . . .

Determination of the right to refuse treatment in anorexia generally hinges on four elements: the anorexic's physical state and the potential risks of her condition; the likely benefit of treatment; the likely harm of treatment; and the competence of the anorexic to make the choice of treatment refusal.

In evaluating *potential risks* of the anorexic's condition, it is important to realize that premature death is a very real possibility in anorexia. When the anorexic shows signs of severe emaciation and physical deterioration, it is the medical practitioner, if the anorexic is being seen by one, who must decide whether hospitalization is required, even against the patient's will. Joel Yager, an eating disorder psychiatrist and professor, recommends refraining from considering legal means of treatment imposition—involuntary hospitalization—unless treatment refusal is judged to constitute a serious risk. The potential for death is certainly a risk serious enough to warrant consideration of involuntary hospitalization. However, premature death in anorexia generally results from cardiac failure which cannot usually be predicted. It is also estimated that from one-third to one-half of premature deaths in anorexia are due to suicide.

More Harm than Good

Potential benefit or harm as a result of treatment also needs to be considered. While generally treatment of anorexia results in improvement, these results are debatable for sufferers of extreme, chronic anorexia. How humane is it to intervene with someone whose physical deterioration will prevent her from ever returning to normal life? Chronic anorexia leads to loneliness, isolation, and stunted development emotionally, physically, socially and vocationally. It has been noted that the anorexic's "rigid control of all aspects of life tends to kill life as other people know it, and indeed as the patient herself has known it." To what degree is this reversible? Or can we assume that there is always at least the possibility that quality of life will improve, even if only marginally so? There are cases where long-term sufferers of anorexia have made remarkable recovery, generally where starvation has not caused serious damage to vital organs or systems. Also, there certainly are situations where some kind of forced nutrition has resulted in the anorexic's later improvement; but in others this has not been true. There are also cases in which chronic anorexics have been, perhaps mistakenly, labeled "incurable." In Great Britain, treatment of a 24-year-old anorexic was deemed "futile" and her condition "incurable." The young woman was admitted into a terminal care facility where she received morphine injections and died after eight days. The anorexic's records were reviewed after her death by a special interest group at the Royal College of Psychiatrists, and the psychiatrists concluded that the patient in fact had likely *not been* incurable. Ethical concerns such as those raised by these cases must be considered in choosing how to proceed.

In the case of chronic anorexia, however, sometimes the pain of continuing life is more than the anorexic can bear; the prospect of any significant recovery is grim and the ordeal of struggling to continue a miserable existence is overwhelming. Often the anorexic who reaches this stage has experienced several hospitalizations or may even currently be in the hospital and refusing treatment. If legal authorization has been obtained, medical staff can tube feed a hospitalized anorexic, but anorexics have been known to tear out the tubes. Treatment can actually be potentially damaging if aggressive or intrusive feeding measures are used. Yager notes that when the willing cooperation of the anorexic is absent, treatments based on invasive feeding are usually short-lived and likely to fail. There is also the issue of what constitutes quality of life: If increasingly aggressive measures are required to prolong an anorexic's life, her physical and psychological capacities certainly will deteriorate. In addition, few facilities can treat these patients indefinitely, and families can rarely pay for prolonged care. In these instances, Yager poses the question: "How long can or should such drawn-out suicides or dying processes continue?" The most humane stance for the clinician at this point may be to help the family develop compassion and understanding for

Gratitude After Compulsory Treatment

It has been argued that the gratitude afterwards of patient and parents would speak for compulsory treatment. This reminds of methodological flaws of many patients' satisfaction studies with involuntary admission and compulsory treatment, which were conducted while patients were still under commitment. As one cannot overrule a competent patient's decision on the chance that the person might be grateful later, this argument assumes incompetence of the patient.

Günther Rathner,
"A Plea Against Compulsory Treatment
of Anorexia Nervosa Patients," in Treating Eating Disorders:
Ethical, Legal and Personal Issues, *eds. Walter Vandereycken*
and Pierre J.V. Beumont. London, UK: Athlone Press, 1998.

the anorexic's perspective and to prepare everyone involved for the possibility or even likelihood of a fatal outcome.

There are other situations where treatment can create more harm than good. In a hospital or outpatient setting where staff members do not understand the plight of the severely ill anorexic or do not know how to work with her, staff may become angry about the way she is manipulative or not trying to get better. An anorexic who feels blamed for her condition is likely to experience further psychological distress, which can make her more resistant to making use of the available help. Even an experienced clinician can become discouraged at a client's lack of progress or apparently oppositional behavior, and may withdraw or disengage from the anorexic. Working successfully with an anorexic whose illness is either severe or long-standing requires considerable patience, compassion, empathy and fortitude.

Competence to Make Choices

The question of an *anorexic's competence to make choices* about her own health care is complicated. The anorexic doubtless chose to lose weight initially. However, starvation leads to psychological and biological consequences over which the anorexic has no control. Her mental distortion may preclude her from comprehending the extent of her medical danger. Also, she probably is more afraid of treatment than of continuing to live as she has been living—marginally, starving, weak, but still under the impression that somehow she is in control. Her eating disorder is her trusted safety net; the specter of treatment is tantamount to prison.

Criteria that indicate that the anorexic is *not* competent to make decisions on her own behalf include a distinct inability to communicate choices, to understand relevant information, and to appreciate the severity of her situation and its consequences. This assessment mostly rests on the anorexic's capacity to take rational steps to preserve her health and life. While the anorexic may be lucid in respect to other aspects of life, anorexia can disable her capacity to make a free and rational decision about the condition itself. An anorexic can sincerely declare her *intention* to resume eating, but when actually faced with food, she may be fraught with anxiety stemming from the thought disturbances of anorexia. Research clinicians [J.] Tiller, [U.] Schmidt and [J.] Treasure note that "the desire, when emaciated, to avoid treatment leading to weight gain is not comparable to a decision to refuse medical intervention; rather it is a psychiatric symptom."

> "For parents, [family-based therapy is]
> a glimmer of hope for a serious illness
> still lacking a gold-standard treatment."

Family Therapy Is an Effective Treatment for Anorexia

Julie Deardorff

In the following viewpoint, Julie Deardorff claims that family-based therapy, or the Maudsley approach, holds promise for treating anorexia, especially in adolescents. In the first phase of this method, she explains, parents take control of "re-feeding" their child—as the lack of nourishment disturbs his or her ability to think rationally—until a healthy body weight is restored and eventually control can be returned to the child. Deardorff claims that clinical evidence supports the effectiveness of family-based therapy in the initial treatment of anorexia, but that it requires constant supervision and dedication from parents and is not suited for all patients. The author is a reporter for the Chicago Tribune.

As you read, consider the following questions:

1. What is the final phase of family-based treatment, according to Deardorff?

2. What do critics say about forcing adolescents to relinquish their power over food, as stated by Deardorff?

3. What does a weight gain of three to four pounds indicate, as claimed by Daniel Le Grange?

War broke out on the day Rina Ranalli and her husband told their 12-year-old anorexic daughter the strict new house rules: three meals and three snacks a day.

Initially, their bright and previously sweet-natured girl cried, screamed insults and raged. She threw things. Punched holes in the wall. And she pretended to eat while plotting ways to hide the food. But when the seventh-grader realized her parents had her trapped—they would sit with her 24/7 if they had to—she ventured down the only available path. She began eating.

Chicago's Ranalli family was using the little-known Maudsley approach, a grueling but evidence-based treatment for adolescents suffering from the eating disorder anorexia nervosa. The approach, also called "family-based therapy," flips conventional treatment on its head.

Often parents are advised to put their starving child in therapy or residential treatment, distance themselves to preserve the teen's independence and wait for the day the child decides to resume eating.

But under Maudsley, parents immediately start the daunting task of "re-feeding" their malnourished child. Once weight is restored—and, theoretically, rational thinking returns because the brain has some nourishment—parents step back, and control over eating is gradually returned to the child. The final phase of treatment is the initial step in traditional therapy; it addresses the underlying psychological issues that may have caused the disorder.

Part of the Solution

Critics of the approach say forcing adolescents to relinquish their power over food can exacerbate underlying control issues. They question whether Maudsley teaches children how to eat intuitively. And they wonder whether parents are equipped for the harrowing and relentless task of getting a child to finally eat.

But Maudsley has something other remedies for anorexia do not: A modest body of clinical evidence suggesting that most adolescent patients respond favorably after relatively few treatment sessions. For parents, it's a glimmer of hope for a serious illness still lacking a gold-standard treatment.

"If you just Google 'eating disorder' and 'anorexia,' you feel like you've been handed a death sentence," said Ranalli, whose already slender daughter (whom they didn't want named) lost 16 pounds in six weeks. "You cry a lot. Maudsley reassures you that it's not your fault and empowered us; we were part of the solution."

Anorexia is unusual in that sufferers often see the illness as an ally. They have a morbid fear of fatness and think about food obsessively; they may cook extravagant meals for others or longingly gaze at food in the grocery store. But they don't eat.

Social isolation is common. When Emily Troscianko, 26, made the decision to eat more after living with her anorexia for 10 years, "it felt like I was bidding goodbye to my closest, most loyal friend," wrote Troscianko, the author of the *Psychology Today* blog *A Hunger Artist*.

The disorder runs in families and is associated with perfectionism, said Dr. Walter [H.] Kaye, the director of the eating disorder treatment and research program at the University of California, San Diego.

"Those with anorexia tend to pay precise attention to detail. They want to do things right. They're achievement-oriented and have advantages in engineering, medicine and academics," said Kaye, whose research focuses on the brain and eating behavior. "Perhaps the illness is caused by an excessive load of traits, puberty and hormones, environment or stress. We're still trying to figure it all out."

Boosting a Child's Chance

Eating disorders are difficult to treat in part because they're hard to study. They're still relatively rare—affecting an estimated 2 percent of U.S. women and 1 percent of men—and it's not easy recruiting research subjects, who rarely want to be treated in the first place.

Just five randomized, controlled studies have examined the treatment of anorexia in adolescents, according to Daniel Le Grange, director of the eating disorders program at the University of Chicago Medical Center. Four of the five published studies include family-based therapy, or the Maudsley approach.

Though the studies are small, they indicate that early treatment with Maudsley boosts a child's chance of getting a handle on the illness. Maudsley has also been found to be effective for those who don't yet have full-blown anorexia but are teetering on the edge.

"A weight gain of 3 to 4 pounds in the first month of treatment gives an 80 percent certainty of good outcome," said Le Grange, a professor of psychiatry and behavioral neuroscience who helped develop the approach at London's Maudsley Hospital and brought the treatment to the U.S.

The success rate drops considerably for children who don't quickly gain weight during treatment. But Le Grange argues that given Maudsley's promising results—and limited comparative data—the family-based treatment should be the first-line intervention instead of an alternative for adolescents who qualify for outpatient care.

"To be really honest with families, we should say: 'We only have one treatment. There is a fair amount of evidence, and it's what you should start with,'" Le Grange said. "If clinicians are not willing to do that, then we have to agree we're just improvising."

After Ranalli's daughter was diagnosed in February 2008, the family spent seven months using more traditional methods, including a therapist and nutritionist. "It was painfully slow," Ranalli said. "So much is left back to the adolescent, waiting for them to come along."

"A Matter of Wills"

Maudsley generally involves 20 sessions over a six- to 12-month period. No one shoulders the blame, and families learn to separate the illness from the child. It's not that the child won't eat; it's that the illness has taken over and won't let them.

"The disease is calling the shots, starving her, making her depressed, obsessive, unable to sleep and compulsively exercise, so parents do need to take control," said Jane Cawley, co-founder of the support group Maudsley Parents. "It seems awful and strange—like you're making your kid suffer—but the whole goal was to get her back in charge of her life."

Family meals are a crucial component of the process. The first takes place with a therapist present to help coach. After that, families are in charge of feeding their child an astonishingly high number of calories a day—often twice what a healthy person would need—to get the weight back on.

Rather than emotional pleas, parents are asked to use empathic but firm declarative statements, such as "I'm no longer going to let you starve," "This is your medicine" and "I won't give up," said Katharine Loeb, an associate professor in the school of psychology at Fairleigh Dickinson University. She is also director of the eating and weight disorders program at the Mount Sinai School of Medicine.

The Meaning of "Family" in Family Therapy

The meaning of 'family' in the context of this treatment approach is quite broad and not strictly dictated by biology or law. The family engaged in the Maudsley approach can be defined as narrowly as the affected teen's parent(s), or broadly to encompass stepparents, long-term significant others, siblings, grandparents, aunts, uncles or others. The therapist will expect to meet with everyone who lives with the individual with the eating disorder. In addition, people who are involved in caring for or feeding the individual, but who do not live with the individual with the eating disorder, will also be required to participate in the treatment. Enlisting the help of all caregivers is essential—for example, grandparents who watch their grandchild after school—and these caregivers are typically required to join a few sessions to learn more about the Maudsley approach. Most important is to utilise such meetings to make sure that everyone is on 'the same page' with one another in the way that the disorder is viewed and treated. Siblings play an important role, but one that is different from that of their parents. Whereas parents' main focus, at least initially, is on weight restoration, siblings are encouraged not to get involved in the parents' efforts, but rather think of ways in which they can support their sibling outside mealtimes; for example, watching a movie together, playing computer games or just having a talk.

June Alexander and Daniel Le Grange,
My Kid Is Back: Empowering Parents to Beat Anorexia Nervosa.
Melbourne, Australia: Melbourne University Press, 2009.

During this challenging first phase, normal life stops until the sufferer eats. Parents may quit jobs, take leaves, cancel all social engagements. It's lonely and exhausting for everyone.

"It's a matter of wills," said Ranalli, who ate lunch with her daughter at school to make sure the girl wasn't throwing the food away. "As a parent you are stating, 'I'm not leaving, I'm not caving, I'm not negotiating. We are not leaving this table until you eat.'

"God, we went through a lot. But you'd do the same in a heartbeat if your child had cancer."

For Nate Schnur, 18, of Wheaton, who was diagnosed with anorexia in August 2009—a week before he was to leave for college—the family meal was a watershed moment. During the lunch, a therapist told him he wouldn't be able to exercise until his weight was restored. Schnur, who worked out compulsively, began to cry.

"The exercise component was Nathan's form of bulimia," said Schnur's mother, Jacqui. "Taking that away from him was our way of 're-feeding' him, in a sense."

The morning after his first family meal, Schnur said he woke up, "freaked out for half an hour" and then ate pancakes. He gained 30 pounds in three weeks—eating mostly fast food—and is in the final phase of Maudsley.

"I didn't want to worry anymore; I just wanted to enjoy my food," said Schnur, who is headed to Loyola University Chicago in the fall. "I was always thinking about how much I could eat or not. But once I started eating, I really noticed how my mind didn't focus on food and working out."

A Ongoing Process

Some critics of Maudsley question the long-term effectiveness of such a controlling approach, especially with teens. "Taking food completely out of their control could give the message they can't be trusted or can't trust themselves, which might be problematic long term," said Jennifer Schurman, a counselor at the Awakening Center in Chicago who specializes in eating disorders.

And Maudsley isn't the answer for everyone. It's virtually impossible if parents don't agree on the approach. Families who use it often say they need more guidance, support and resources, especially in a single-parent household.

And even when there's success, as with the Ranalli family, making peace with food is an ongoing process.

"I still have body issues," the Ranallis' daughter, now 15, said while sipping a light coffee Frappuccino at a Chicago Starbucks. "But the thing that has really changed is that I like food again."

"*What most eating disorder patients do not recognize is that the very act of trying to avoid internal distress keeps them trapped in a self-perpetuating cycle.*"

Acceptance and Commitment Therapy Is an Effective Treatment for Eating Disorders

Kathy Kater

Kathy Kater is a psychotherapist specializing in eating and body image and the author of Healthy Body Image: Teaching Kids to Eat and Love Their Bodies Too! *In the following viewpoint, Kater insists that acceptance and commitment therapy (ACT) can aid in the recovery of eating disorders. Accepting—not challenging—the obsessive, destructive thoughts of anorexia or bulimia can enable patients to see them as "just thoughts" and respond in constructive ways, she maintains. Through ACT, patients can also learn to view their selves and their thoughts in a larger context, Kater continues, and ultimately connect with their deepest values and purpose in life.*

Kathy Kater, "A New Approach for Treating Eating Disorders: Acceptance and Commitment Therapy (ACT)," *Eating Disorders Recovery Today*, vol. 7, Fall 2009. © 2009 Gürze Books. All rights reserved. Reproduced by permission of Gürze Books, LLC.

As you read, consider the following questions:

1. What are eating disorder thoughts, as described by the author?

2. What example does Kater provide of "mindfulness" at work?

3. In the author's opinion, why is ACT a challenging form of treatment?

While the medical consequences of an eating disorder can be life threatening, the unrelenting internal dialogue and the compulsion to follow rules and rituals causes most of the suffering. The endless stream of fear-based judgments, rigid demands, and threats can take over a mind and sometimes drive a life into the ground. It is in the face of these "eating disorder thoughts" and the difficult emotions and impulses they provoke that patients must triumph if they are to begin the long road to recovery. Even those who interrupt eating disorder behaviors for weeks, months, or even years remain vulnerable to a re-arising of powerful mental formations that may trigger a relapse.

While it is always tempting to appeal to reason and logic to challenge self-destructive thinking—the goal of Cognitive Behavioral Therapy (CBT)—as a seasoned therapist I have not found entrenched eating disorder thoughts to be significantly diminished by rational arguments or objective evidence. Recently, I discovered that the compelling methods of Acceptance and Commitment Therapy (ACT) describe and enhance an approach that I have found works better in helping eating disorder patients move toward recovery.

Acceptance and Commitment Therapy

ACT does not attempt to change the *content* of irrational or negative thoughts and difficult emotions, even if this is false and destructive. Instead the goal is to help people *face* these thoughts, *see* them from a different perspective, and in turn *respond* in a way that is more helpful.

Research has demonstrated that ACT is highly effective with disorders that are driven by *experiential avoidance*: a compelling urge to avoid or control difficult internal states such as unpleasant or painful thoughts, emotions, or sensations. While studies using ACT for treating eating disorders have not yet been done, these are certainly driven by a powerful compulsion to get rid of or control disturbing mind and body states. For example, eating disorder sufferers routinely deal with thoughts such as "I'm too fat" (and therefore out of control or unacceptable), or body states like a full stomach by using eating disorder behaviors to temporarily reduce distress or feel in control.

What most eating disorder patients do not recognize is that the very act of trying to avoid internal distress keeps them trapped in a self-perpetuating cycle. Like a Chinese finger trap, the harder we try to escape, the more we are locked in. Repeatedly running away from difficult emotions, whether by not eating, purging, drinking alcohol, or any other "fix," only creates more problems by creating a dependency on avoidance behaviors and teaching nothing about coping with the inevitable difficulties of life.

Acceptance

Helping patients become willing to face their difficult thoughts is the "acceptance" part of ACT. We might say, "Ok, you think you are fat and disgusting." Even though we do not agree with this thought and consider it harmful, we do not argue with or challenge it. Instead ACT uses mindfulness and cognitive defusion methods to help people mentally "step back" and see this thought for what it is: *just a thought*, i.e., the firing of certain synapses in the brain that may or may not be helpful. Eating disorder thoughts are mental constructions that have formed as a result of separate thoughts and events that have become associated and that are now triggered involuntarily and *as if they were one*. For example, therapists often hear how associations between feeling bad, not eating, and in some way feeling better or "in control" can be traced to an event such as this one:

> "Right after he broke up with me he started dating the skinniest girl in our class. I felt so bad, I could hardly eat. When I started to lose weight it felt good when people complimented me. That's when I started to restrict on purpose, and the more weight I lost the better I felt. It was like the one thing I could do to feel in control."

When thoughts are associated, separate thoughts and the impulses they bring up can become *fused*, as if they were one and the same. Thereafter, whenever any part of this thought is triggered, the entire "fused thought" arises. For example, once eating behaviors have been associated with stress relief, any experience of angst may trigger an eating disorder thought like this: *feeling anxious, can't stand it, don't eat, feel better*. At this point, the world as colored by this thought seems so real, it's as if the person is no longer interacting with thoughts at all. Instead eating/not eating has become a life or death reality.

Facing Eating Disorder Thoughts

Just as getting out of quicksand requires a counterintuitive action, facing eating disorder thoughts without obeying them can seem impossible. Yet it is the only alternative to being enslaved. Once they exist, eating disorder thoughts and impulses cannot be willfully stopped from arising. What is possible is to learn to look *at* thoughts instead of viewing the world *from* them.

Mindfulness is a two-millennium-old method for creating this distance and objectivity. Mindfulness makes it possible to become aware that in any present moment there is a "me" that is thinking and a "me" that can "watch myself think." When patients first experience this, I often ask them, "*Who is watching?*" When they become curious about this *observing self*—a self that transcends their thinking mind—they can see that it is possible to view both their self and their thoughts within a bigger context than they previously knew, creating a space in which new possibilities can arise.

Research has documented that the perspective from which thoughts are viewed can significantly alter their impact. For example, a patient told me, "*I can't stand to feel full—it makes me feel like I will blow up!*" When fused with this thought, it seemed literally true to her. From her perspective, eating until full was akin to annihilation! Using mindfulness she was able to learn to observe this thought instead of being caught in it, and it became possible for her to say "*I'm having the thought that if I feel full I will explode.*"

In the space that opened she had room to feel sad that the years of eating only morsels in order to obey this thought had cost her many of her dreams. In her case, being a slave to eating disorder rules had forced her to withdraw from training as a potential Olympic skater. From this new vantage point she could begin to consider whether she might be willing to have this thought, and even tolerate the anxiety it evoked, if it meant she could begin to follow new dreams, such as becoming a skating teacher.

Connecting with an Ultimate Purpose

In line with this, another goal of ACT is helping patients to connect with their deepest values and ultimate purpose in life. What else could generate a willingness to face what torments us and to let go of behaviors that provide an illusion of control? By connecting with values, patients become aware of what they would want to be able to say about their life if their eating disorder thoughts and impulses were not controlling their actions: "*In a world where you could choose to have your life be about something, what would you choose?*" When patients feel immobilized on the difficult road to recovery, values clarification shines a compelling light on why they must go on.

ACT's overall therapeutic goal is to help patients ride out the inevitable waves of emotionally provocative thoughts and impulses while committing to actions that align with what really matters most in their lives. ACT is challenging because it conflicts with some of the basic tenets of Western thought, such as that "pain is bad," "happiness depends on feeling good ('feel-goodism')," and "if you just work hard enough you can get whatever you want." Therapists are hooked by these beliefs in ways that are not all that different from our patients—I know I have been. It has taken me time and practice to integrate ACT into my work. To apply it I must continually ask myself, "What do *I* do when faced with pain?" The results have been professionally and personally rewarding.

"Regardless of the mechanism of action of antidepressants in treating bulimia, they are effective agents, at least for short-term treatment and in many instances for up to several years."

Antidepressants Are Effective in the Treatment of Bulimia

Michael J. Gitlin

Michael J. Gitlin is a clinical psychiatry professor at the University of California, Los Angeles, School of Medicine. In the following viewpoint, excerpted from his book The Psychotherapist's Guide to Psychopharmacology, *Gitlin asserts that antidepressants can be effective in treating bulimia. According to him, their efficacy in decreasing the binge-purge cycle has been documented in short-term treatment studies, and when one antidepressant fails, another will often work. Several explanations for the mechanism of action of antidepressants in bulimia include the prevalence of depression in bulimic patients, antidepressants' therapeutic anti-anxiety properties, and their effects on neurotransmitters that regulate appetite, Gitlin claims.*

As you read, consider the following questions:

1. How does Gitlin back his proposition that bulimia is possibly a variant of depression?

2. What is the first important point therapists must acknowledge about medication and bulimia, in the author's opinion?

3. What fears and resistances may bulimic patients have of antidepressants, as stated by Gitlin?

Those with bulimia share with anorexic patients the over-concern with body shape and size. The hallmark of bulimia, however, is the repetitive cycle of out-of-control binge eating alternating with a variety of behaviors that attempt to undo the effects of the binging, such as self-induced vomiting, laxative abuse, fasting, or vigorous exercising. Patients can simultaneously have anorexia and bulimia. The majority of patients who present for treatment, however, have normal-weight bulimia.

In contrast to anorexia nervosa, medications—specifically antidepressants—have documented efficacy in decreasing the binge-purge cycle in short-term treatment studies. Compared to those treated with placebo, bulimic patients on antidepressants will show a greater decrease in binge frequency, with that decrease averaging 75 percent across studies. A variety of antidepressants have been utilized with the majority showing positive results. These have included the tricyclic antidepressants, such as imipramine and desipramine, the newer antidepressants, trazodone and fluoxetine, as well as the monoamine oxidase inhibitors. There is no substantive evidence that one antidepressant has significantly greater efficacy than the others. Often, when one antidepressant is ineffective, a different one will work, so that several trials are warranted in the patient who fails to respond to the first antidepressant prescribed. Antidepressant doses in treating bulimia are the same as those for depression, and the time course to response—up to six weeks for a maximum response—is also similar. The other major class of medications that have been used in treating bulimia are the anticonvulsants such as phenytoin (Dilantin) and carbamazepine (Tegretol). Significant evidence for their efficacy, however, is lacking.

A Variant of Depression

How can we best understand the mechanism of action of antidepressants in bulimia? A number of possible explanations should be considered, no one of which is definitive. The most popular is that bulimia is an unusual variant of depression. Bulimic patients tend to show increased rates of depression both while binge eating and over a lifetime. There is also some evidence, although not entirely consistent, that the families of bulimic patients show a high prevalence of depression, implying some sort of familial and possibly genetic link. That antidepressants are so helpful in decreasing core bulimic symptoms could also be interpreted as evidence for bulimia being a "masked depression." Yet on further investigation, this hypothesis—that bulimia and depression are equivalent—is shaky. Sources of dysphoria in bulimic patients are multiple: Depression is mixed with dysphoric mood stemming from poor self-esteem and shame due to the bulimia along with other characterological sources of depressed mood. The marked shifts in weight seen in normal-weight bulimia may also cause some of the biological characteristics of starvation, thereby causing depressive symptoms analogous to those seen in anorexia nervosa. Furthermore, the presence of depression in bulimic patients does not predict a better response to antidepressants in controlling binge frequency. Depression and bulimia, when they coexist, do not necessarily remit together, at times the binging may respond to treatment while the depression continues, while at other times the reverse sequence is seen. Overall, then, conceptualizing bulimia and depression as a single

Guidelines for Considering Medications in Treating Bulimia

Patient has moderate to severe current major depressive disorder

History of recurrent depression when not bulimic

Strong family history of primary depression

Patient has not improved from a well-designed treatment program not involving pharmacotherapy

Michael J. Gitlin,
The Psychotherapist's Guide to Psychopharmacology.
New York: Simon & Schuster, 2007.

disorder with multiple manifestations seems inaccurate. What is more likely is that the two disorders are commonly occurring comorbid conditions, that is, that the presence of one condition (bulimia) makes the presence of the other (depression) most likely, analogous to the frequent co-occurrence of depression and borderline personality disorder. (The reverse sequence—that depressed patients are generally at higher risk to develop bulimia—is probably not true.) Conceptualizing bulimia and depression as separate conditions that are seen together with regularity has important implications in deciding when to introduce antidepressants in treating bulimic patients.

Other Possible Explanations

Another possible explanation for the effect of antidepressants in treating bulimia is related to the antianxiety properties of these medications. Bulimic patients often describe an increasing tension that culminates in a binge-purge cycle. Any treatment—including medications—that can diminish this tension may be associated with decreased binge frequency. No evidence supporting or negating this hypothesis currently exists.

Finally, since antidepressants have effects on those neurotransmitters that are involved with regulation of appetite, it is possible that the decrease in binging is due to the effects of medications on brain regulatory systems. Here too, this hypothesis has no significant experimental support.

Regardless of the mechanism of action of antidepressants in treating bulimia, they are effective agents, at least for short-term treatment and in many instances for up to several years. Some studies indicate a significant rate of relapse when medication is withdrawn, others find no evidence of a medication effect in long-term outcome. Additionally, side effects often become an increased problem following the initial treatment, especially with MAO [monoamine oxidase] inhibitors: consequently many patients stop the medication after months of treatment.

What Therapists Should Consider

Given the information just reviewed, what guidelines should a therapist use in considering the referral of a bulimic patient for possible antidepressant treatment? The first important point is to acknowledge that medications are far from being the only well-documented treatment for bulimia. A variety of psychological approaches utilizing cognitive, behavioral, educational, psychodynamic, and supportive techniques in both individual and group formats have shown clear evidence of efficacy. Second, studies comparing antidepressants to educational/cognitive/behavioral approaches are rare. Third, medications are sometimes difficult to use in bulimic patients: side effects are often problematic, affecting compliance; vomiting can cause erratic medication blood levels, making pharmacotherapy inconsistent; and the necessary dietary restrictions with the MAO inhibitors make these particular medications acceptable for only a subset of those with bulimia. Finally, there are no established predictors for antidepressant responses with bulimic patients.

Before suggesting the exploration of possible medication approaches with the patient, a clinician must first pay attention to the possible fears and resistances involved. Since issues of control are so central to bulimia, patients often are frightened of being addicted to medications and are concerned that taking medication is an indication of lack of self-control. Bulimics also fear that the medications will make them fat. . . .

Although the presence of depression does not predict a better anti-bulimic response to antidepressants, the medications may nonetheless successfully treat an associated depression, if present. The alleviation of the depression is likely to help the patient work more productively in any other treatment modality by increasing concentration and energy and by combating pessimism, negative expectation, and helplessness while promoting a general sense of well-being.

Since, as mentioned above, the multiple sources of depressive symptoms in bulimic patients sometimes blur the distinctions among these overlapping diagnoses, a history of depressions when the patient was not bulimic suggests that she is at high risk for a difficult-to-recognize major depressive episode which may then complicate the treatment of the bulimia. A strong family history of depression has similar implications. Finally, since there are no established predictors for response to any treatment for bulimia, the last guideline stresses the empirical nature of treatment planning. If the patient continues to binge and purge despite active participation in a multimodal treatment program, the addition of antidepressants may be very helpful.

> *"Since binge eaters have highly irregular eating habits, the behavioral aspect introduces structure to their eating behavior: regular meals, including breakfast, and an afternoon snack if needed."*

A Structured Eating Plan Can Control Binge Eating

Jane E. Brody

In the following viewpoint, Jane E. Brody writes that binge eating disorder (BED) can be managed with a structured eating plan and behavioral changes. Brody retells her battle with bingeing, which she overcame by creating an eating plan for herself that stressed regular meals. Brody states that according to experts, her "cure" is similar to the therapeutic measures used to help patients with BED. In addition, cognitive behavioral therapy (CBT) can counter unhealthy thoughts about food and eating as a response to emotional problems, Brody maintains. The author is the Personal Health columnist for the New York Times.

As you read, consider the following questions:

1. As described by Brody, what was her eating program?

2. What are the main goals of therapy for binge eating, as claimed in the viewpoint?

3. What meal plan is effective in stopping bingeing and starting weight loss, as described by the author?

This month [February 2007], researchers at Harvard published a survey finding that binge eating is by far the most common eating disorder, occurring in 1 in 35 adults, or 2.8 percent—almost twice the combined rate for anorexia (0.6 percent) and bulimia (1 percent).

Yet unlike the other two, binge eating disorder is still not considered a formal diagnosis by the American Psychiatric Association. I'm mystified as to why, and when you read my story you may wonder as well.

It was 1964, I was 23 and working at my first newspaper job in Minneapolis, 1,250 miles from my New York home. My love life was in disarray, my work was boring, my boss was a misogynist. And I, having been raised to associate love and happiness with food, turned to eating for solace.

Of course, I began to gain weight and, of course, I periodically went on various diets to try to lose what I'd gained, only to relapse and regain all I'd lost and then some.

My many failed attempts included the Drinking Man's Diet, popular at the time, which at least enabled me to stay connected with my hard-partying colleagues.

Before long, desperation set in. When I found myself unable to stop eating once I'd started, I resolved not to eat during the day. Then, after work and out of sight, the bingeing began.

I learned where the few all-night mom-and-pop shops were located so I could pick up the evening's supply on my way home from work. Then I would spend the night eating nonstop, first something sweet, then something salty, then back to sweet, and so on. A half-gallon of ice cream was only the beginning. I was capable of consuming 3,000 calories at a sitting. Many mornings I awakened to find partly chewed food still in my mouth.

And, as you might expect, because I didn't purge (never even heard of it then), I got fatter and fatter until I had gained a third more than my normal body weight, even though I was physically active.

My despair was profound, and one night in the midst of a binge I became suicidal. I had lost control of my eating; it was controlling me, and I couldn't go on living that way.

Fortunately, I was still rational enough to reach out for help, and at 2 a.m. I called a psychologist I knew at his home. His willingness to see me in the morning got me through the night.

Just talking about my behavior and learning from the psychologist that I was not the only person with this problem helped relieve my despair. Still, he was not able to help me stop bingeing. That was something I would have to do on my own.

I finally reached the conclusion that if I kept eating that way, the dreadful foods would end up killing me. And I knew by then that diets were a disaster, something one goes on to go off, only to regain what one has lost. So I decided that if I was going to be fat, at least I was going to be healthy.

An Eating Plan

With my then limited knowledge of nutrition, I created an eating program for myself: three substantial meals a day with a wholesome snack between meals if I was hungry. No skipping meals allowed. I stripped my apartment of favorite binge foods, though I allowed myself one small treat a day. And I continued with my regular physical activity.

After a month of eating three big meals a day, I had lost seven pounds. And I continued to lose about two pounds a month (as my weight dropped, so did the amount of food I needed to feel satisfied) until two years later I was back to my normal weight.

As I have learned from talking with experts who treat eating disorders, the factors that precipitated my binge eating and the route I took to "cure" myself are strikingly similar to the precipitants among their binge-eating patients and the therapeutic measures used to help them.

It is important for everyone out there with this problem to know that help is available.

While binge eating without purging occurs in 2.8 percent of the adult population, it is much more prevalent, as you might expect, in obese people.

Dr. Katherine Halmi, director of the eating disorders program at the Westchester division of New York-Presbyterian Hospital, says 10 percent to 15 percent of the obese population has this problem, and among those who binge without purging, almost 90 percent are obese.

Dr. Halmi, who is also a professor of psychiatry at the Weill Cornell Medical College in New York, said she had found dieting a frequent "proximal trigger" among people with binge eating disorder.

Other common risk factors, Dr. Halmi said, include a "personal disaster in a person's life, like the death of a spouse, losing one's job, having a serious problem at work, or being left by one's husband for another woman."

"People soon learn that binge eating alleviates anxiety, similar to an addiction," she said. "There's psychological reinforcement of the behavior because binge eating makes them feel better at the time, even though they may feel upset afterward for having eaten so much."

Dr. B. Timothy Walsh, an eating disorders specialist at the New York State Psychiatric Institute at Columbia University Medical Center, says that when compared with equally

Treating Binge Eating in the Absence of Obesity

Even in the absence of obesity, patients suffering from binge eating disorder seek and merit treatment because they experience significant distress over their loss of control with respect to eating binges and because they experience significant distress, including feeling disgust, guilt, or depression, after overeating. In addition, as previously mentioned, associated psychiatric and medical comorbidities often add to their plight.

Joel Yager,
"Binge Eating Disorder: The Search for Better Treatments,"
American Journal of Psychiatry, *vol. 165, January 1, 2008.*

overweight people who do not binge, binge eaters are more troubled by anxiety and depression.

Getting Help

The main goals of therapy are abstinence from binge eating, and weight loss or weight control, said Cynthia M. Bulik, the distinguished professor of eating disorders in the psychiatry department at the University of North Carolina at Chapel Hill. Dr. Walsh adds that emotional relief is another goal, and that it sometimes results from achieving the other two.

Most popular at the moment is cognitive behavioral therapy, with or without medication. Since binge eaters have highly irregular eating habits, the behavioral aspect introduces structure to their eating behavior: regular meals, including breakfast, and an afternoon snack if needed.

Dr. Halmi said those in recovery must not go more than four hours without eating, and that their diet should include foods they like.

The cognitive aspect tries to undo the unhealthy notions people have about food and eating, like "I've already blown it, so I might as well eat the rest of the ice cream" or "I didn't eat breakfast, so I can eat more at night."

"We also help them find more appropriate responses to emotional problems, like using relaxation techniques instead of food to deal with anxiety," Dr. Bulik said.

The cognitive behavioral approach, while highly effective in stopping binge eating, is less effective in achieving weight loss, she said.

Thomas Wadden, director of the Center for Weight and Eating Disorders at the University of Pennsylvania, has found that "a behavioral weight control approach"—a structured meal plan that reduces daily intake by 500 to 700 calories but allows a couple hundred calories from foods the person likes—is effective in stopping bingeing and also helps the person lose weight.

"We see an improvement in people's moods," Dr. Wadden said, adding that there should also be therapy to deal with relationship issues or self-esteem, if needed.

Medication is also sometimes used with the structured eating plan. Prozac and similar antidepressants and the anticonvulsant drug Topamax have helped some patients gain control of their weight and achieve abstinence from bingeing, Dr. Bulik said, though data are lacking on long-term effectiveness.

As for me, do I still sometimes eat "out of control"? Yes, now and then.

When I feel anxious or upset, I may polish off a dozen innocent-looking cookies or a pint of low-fat ice cream. But this is nothing like it once was. And since 1967, with minor fluctuations, I have stayed at my normal weight.

Periodical and Internet Sources Bibliography

The following articles have been selected to supplement the diverse views presented in this chapter.

Natalya Anderson	"The Maudsley Maintenance Model for Anorexia Nervosa," *Irish Medical Times*, September 17, 2009.
Carrie Arnold	"A Girl's Suffering Drove Her Parents to Explore a New Anorexia Treatment," *Washington Post*, February 24, 2009.
Anna M. Bardone-Cone and Christine R. Maldonado	"Defining What It Means to Be 'Recovered,'" *Eating Disorders Recovery Today*, Summer 2008.
Lauren Brown	"21 Days to Save Her Life," *CosmoGirl!*, February 2007.
Lindsay Bruce	"Ingleby Barwick Teenager on Beating Anorexia," *Evening Gazette*, July 2, 2011.
Erica Garvin	"Renfrew Center: Breaking the Silence," *Inside Healthcare*, December 2010.
Aimee Liu	"The 24-Hour Treatment for Anorexia," *Ms. Magazine Blog*, October 28, 2010. http://msmagazine.com/blog.
Roni Carin Rabin	"Bringing in Family to Combat Anorexia," *New York Times*, October 18, 2010.
Margarita Tartakovsky	"Eating Disorder Recovery: Healing from Within," *Weightless* (blog), December 9, 2010. http://blogs.psychcentral.com.
Mary Ellen Trunko and Walter H. Kaye	"Pharmacological Treatment of Bulimia Nervosa," *Psychiatric Times*, May 2008.

For Further Discussion

Chapter 1

1. Malcolm Evans contends that definitions of eating disorders have become too open. In your opinion, does the Senate Committee on Health, Education, Labor and Pensions use such definitions? Use examples from the viewpoints to support your answer.

2. Tedra Coakley maintains that images of African American women are incorporated in the media to fit the thinness ideals of white women. Do you agree or disagree with the author? Why or why not?

3. Linda Bacon claims that the obesity epidemic is a myth that perpetuates unhealthy ideas about weight. In your view, does Sara Selis promote harmful misperceptions about obesity? Cite examples from the texts to explain your response.

Chapter 2

1. Johanna S. Kandel claims that anorexia and bulimia have a strong genetic basis. On the other hand, Simona Giordano downplays genes in the development of eating disorders, citing environmental influences. In your opinion, who makes the more compelling argument? Provide examples from the viewpoints to support your answer.

2. Julia Cheng suggests that naturally slender women can be unfairly scrutinized because of eating disorders. Do you agree or disagree with the author? Why or why not?

3. Jessica Bennett is concerned that there is a growing, harmful discrepancy between the bodies of fashion models and the average woman. However, Lisa Hilton insists that this discrepancy demonstrates that the average woman has

become heavier and that is the larger problem. In your view, who offers the more persuasive statement? Explain your reasoning.

Chapter 3

1. Jaclyn Gallucci states that some eating disorders websites are pro-recovery and prohibit teaching, tips, and encouragement of eating disorders. In your view, does Lauren Cox's assertion that over 80 percent of pro-recovery sites provide harmful advice weaken Gallucci's position? Cite examples from the texts to explain your response.

2. Virginia Heffernan proposes that thinspiration videos are artistic and personal outlets of expression for individuals with eating disorders. Do you agree or disagree with Heffernan? Why or why not?

3. Adam Thierer argues that regulating pro-anorexia and pro-bulimia sites would drive them underground and limit professionals' access to sufferers of eating disorders. In your opinion, would the suggestions of the Royal College of Psychiatrists to regulate these sites result in this outcome? Provide examples from the viewpoints to support your answer.

Chapter 4

1. Cornelia Thiels declares that involuntary treatment of anorexia is justified. On the other hand, Avis Rumney contends that it would be harmful in the severest cases. In your opinion, which author's position is more ethically sound? Cite examples from the texts to explain your response.

2. In your view, does Michael J. Gitlin make a strong case for the use of antidepressants to treat bulimic patients? Why or why not?

3. Julie Deardorff offers anecdotal evidence for the effectiveness of family-based therapy, including some supporting

studies. In your opinion, is this evidence satisfactory? Use examples from the viewpoint to support your answer.

Organizations to Contact

The editors have compiled the following list of organizations concerned with the issues debated in this book. The descriptions are derived from materials provided by the organizations. All have publications or information available for interested readers. The list was compiled on the date of publication of the present volume; names, addresses, phone and fax numbers, and e-mail and Internet addresses may change. Be aware that many organizations take several weeks or longer to respond to inquiries, so allow as much time as possible.

Academy for Eating Disorders (AED)
111 Deer Lake Road, Suite 100, Deerfield, IL   60015
(847) 498-4274 • fax: (847) 480-9282
website: www.aedweb.org

The Academy for Eating Disorders (AED) is an international organization of eating disorders research, treatment, and education professionals. It fosters education, training, and interdisciplinary dialogue; holds an annual conference; and develops guidelines for clinical treatment practices. For the general public, its website offers archives of AED press releases and position statements, as well as information about research study participation and locating treatment providers. Eight times a year, the AED publishes the *International Journal of Eating Disorders*, containing full-length scholarly articles about the epidemiological and therapeutic aspects of eating disorders.

American Psychological Association (APA)
750 First Street NE, Washington, DC   20002-4242
(800) 374-2721
website: www.apa.org

The American Psychological Association (APA) is a scientific and professional organization that represents psychology in the United States. With 150,000 members, the APA is the largest association of psychologists worldwide. It publishes articles and reports on eating disorders, body image, and other related topics in its numerous journals and provides additional publications including *Body Image, Eating Disorders, and Obesity in Youth: Assessment, Prevention, and Treatment.*

Council of Fashion Designers of America (CFDA)

1412 Broadway, Suite 2006, New York, NY   10018
website: www.cfda.com

The Council of Fashion Designers of America (CFDA) is a nonprofit trade association consisting of more than three hundred of America's foremost fashion and accessory designers. Founded in 1962, the association continues to advance the status of fashion design as a branch of American art and culture, to raise its artistic and professional standards, to define a code of ethical practices of mutual benefit in public and trade relations, and to promote appreciation of the fashion arts through leadership in quality and aesthetic discernment. In 2007, the CFDA created a health initiative to raise awareness of eating disorders in the fashion industry and to change the aesthetic on runways and in magazines from extreme thinness to a more realistic ideal.

Eating Disorders Coalition for Research, Policy and Action (EDC)

720 Seventh Street NW, Suite 300, Washington, DC   20001
(202) 543-9570
e-mail: manager@eatingdisorderscoalition.org
website: www.eatingdisorderscoalition.org

The Eating Disorders Coalition for Research, Policy and Action (EDC) is a nonprofit association of leading eating disorders advocacy groups, research programs, and treatment facilities that seek recognition of eating disorders as a public health priority, more federal funding for research and treatment, and parity in insurance coverage for mental and physical health services. EDC activities focus on influencing members of Congress and other policy makers through briefings and education, support of legislation, and petition drives. At the EDC website, the general public can view reports about pending legislation and health insurance issues; sign up for e-mail updates; and get involved in EDC activities through the EDC Friends and Family Action Council.

Food and Nutrition Information Center (FNIC)
National Agricultural Library, Beltsville, MD   20705
website: http://fnic.nal.usda.gov

This section of the US Department of Agriculture offers a Diet and Disease—Eating Disorders website that includes many links to resource material on anorexia, bulimia, and binge eating; exercise and eating disorders; teens and eating disorders; and dietary and nutrition assistance programs.

Gürze Books, LLC
5145-B Avenida Encinas, Carlsbad, CA   92008
(760) 434-7533
website: www.bulimia.com

Gürze is an independent publisher specializing in eating disorders publications and education since 1980. The company offers a free eating disorders resource catalog that lists books and tapes from more than fifty publishers as well as its own publications; a bimonthly newsletter for clinicians, the *Eating Disorders Review*; a quarterly newsletter for the general public, *Eating Disorders Today*; and a monthly Internet newsletter, *Gürze Books eNewsletter*.

National Association of Anorexia and Associated Disorders (ANAD)
PO Box 640, Naperville, IL   60566
(630) 577-1333
e-mail: anadhelp@anad.org
website: www.anad.org

The National Association of Anorexia and Associated Disorders (ANAD) is a nonprofit, largely volunteer organization founded in 1976 to raise awareness of eating disorders and to promote treatment and recovery. ANAD representatives help sufferers and their families through hotline counseling and online referrals to support groups and treatment professionals. The ANAD website includes links to information about specific disorders, pending legislation, event schedules, and the organization's online newsletter.

National Eating Disorders Association (NEDA)

165 West Forty-Sixth Street, New York, NY   10036
(212) 575-6200
e-mail: info@nationaleatingdisorders.org
website: www.nationaleatingdisorders.org

Formed in 2001 by the merger of Eating Disorders Awareness & Prevention (EDAP) and the American Anorexia Bulimia Association (AABA), the National Eating Disorders Association (NEDA) is the largest nonprofit group in the United States dedicated to eating disorders education, treatment, and prevention. The association provides a toll-free information and referral helpline; sponsors an annual conference for families, educators, and treatment providers; presents awards and research grants; and lobbies legislators to expand public education programs and patient access to treatment facilities. A comprehensive index of free fact sheets is available at its website, and NEDA's online store sells educational videos, books, brochures, posters, and promotional items.

National Institute of Mental Health (NIMH)

Public Information and Communications Branch
Bethesda, MD   20892-9663
(866) 615-6464
e-mail: nimhinfo@nih.gov
website: www.nimh.nih.gov

The National Institute of Mental Health (NIMH), a branch within the US Department of Health and Human Services, is the lead federal agency for research on mental and behavioral disorders, including eating disorders. Recent and brief news articles about eating disorders are posted periodically on the

NIMH website's News Room section, and good descriptions of current government-sponsored eating disorders research studies (including patient recruitment information) are listed on the website's Clinical Trials section.

Renfrew Center Foundation
475 Spring Lane, Philadelphia, PA   19128
(877) 367-3383 • fax: (215) 482-2695
e-mail: info@renfrew.org
website: http://renfrew.org

The foundation is a nonprofit education and research organization founded in 1990 by the Renfrew Center, the nation's first free-standing facility exclusively dedicated to the treatment of eating disorders. To raise public awareness, the foundation conducts educational seminars and sponsors a speaker's bureau. Its website offers education materials; a free newsletter, *Connections*; and a biannual professional journal, *Perspectives*.

Bibliography of Books

Stephanie Covington Armstrong — *Not All Black Girls Know How to Eat: A Story of Bulimia*. Chicago, IL: Lawrence Hill Books, 2009.

Grace Bowman — *Thin*. New York: Penguin Books, 2008.

Harriet Brown — *Brave Girl Eating: A Family's Struggle with Anorexia*. New York: William Morrow, 2010.

Cynthia M. Bulik — *The Woman in the Mirror: How to Stop Confusing What You Look Like with Who You Are*. New York: Walker and Company, 2011.

Joaquín Dosil — *Eating Disorders in Athletes*. Hoboken, NJ: John Wiley & Sons, 2008.

John Evans, Emma Rich, Brian Davies, and Rachel Allwood — *Education, Disordered Eating, and Obesity Discourse: Fat Fabrications*. New York: Routledge, 2008.

Amy Erdman Farrell — *Fat Shame: Stigma and the Fat Body in American Culture*. New York: New York University Press, 2011.

Lesli J. Favor with Kira Freed — *Food as Foe: Nutrition and Eating Disorders*. New York: Marshall Cavendish Benchmark, 2010.

Emily Fox-Kales   *Body Shots: Hollywood and the Culture of Eating Disorders.* Albany: State University of New York Press, 2011.

Sarah Grogan   *Body Image: Understanding Body Dissatisfaction in Men, Women, and Children.* New York: Routledge, 2008.

Trisha Gura   *Lying in Weight: The Hidden Epidemic of Eating Disorders in Adult Women.* New York: HarperCollins, 2007.

Kate Harding and Marianne Kirby   *Lessons from the Fat-o-Sphere: Quit Dieting and Declare a Truce with Your Body.* New York: Perigee Trade, 2009.

David A. Kessler   *The End of Overeating: Taking Control of the Insatiable American Appetite.* New York: Rodale Books, 2009.

Gina Kolata   *Rethinking Thin: The New Science of Weight Loss—and the Myths and Realities of Dieting.* New York: Farrar, Straus and Giroux, 2007.

Aimee Lu   *Gaining: The Truth About Life After Eating Disorders.* New York: Warner Books, 2007.

Gari Meacham   *Truly Fed: Finding Freedom from Disordered Eating.* Kansas City, MO: Beacon Hill Press of Kansas City, 2009.

Gillian
Moore-Groarke

In Search of Thinness: Treating Anorexia and Bulimia: A Multi-Disciplinary Approach. Dublin, Ireland: Currach Press, 2008.

Michelle McNatt
Myers

The Look That Kills: An Anorexic's Addiction to Control. Bloomington, IN: CrossBooks, 2010.

Jane Ogden

The Psychology of Eating: From Healthy to Disordered Behavior. 2nd ed. Malden, MA: Wiley-Blackwell, 2010.

Tamra Orr

When the Mirror Lies: Anorexia, Bulimia, and Other Eating Disorders. Danbury, CT: Franklin Watts, 2007.

Crystal Renn

Hungry: A Young Model's Story of Appetite, Ambition, and the Ultimate Embrace of Curves. New York: Simon & Schuster, 2009.

Paula Saukko

The Anorexic Self: A Personal, Political Analysis of a Diagnostic Discourse. Albany: State University of New York Press, 2008.

Ron Saxen

The Good Eater: The True Story of One Man's Struggle with Binge Eating Disorder. Oakland, CA: New Harbinger Publications, 2007.

Maria Stavrou, ed.

Bulimics on Bulimia. Philadelphia, PA: Jessica Kingsley Publishers, 2008.

Megan Warin

Abject Relations: Everyday Worlds of Anorexia. New Brunswick, NJ: Rutgers University Press, 2010.

Index

A

Abuse histories, 38, 164
Academy for Eating Disorders, 52, 55, 148
Acceptance and commitment therapy (ACT)
    described, 185, 186–187, 187–188, 190
    is effective, 185–190
Addiction, avoidance behaviors, 187
Advertising
    diet products, 83, 86
    Dove's Campaign for Real Beauty, 90, 97–98
    image manipulation and airbrushing, 95–96, 125
    thinness ideals and body image, 36–37, 38, 86
African American women, 32–41
Agency for Healthcare Research and Quality, 55, 57
Airbrushing and image manipulation, 95–96, 125
Alexander, June, 182
Allergies, 29
Alliance for Eating Disorders Awareness, 121
American Heart Association, 103
American Psychiatric Association
    eating disorder diagnoses, 51, 198
    standards of care and treatment, 22
"Ana" websites
    are dangerous, 120–126, 129

contributors, 118, 122, 129, 132, 133–134, 143
critics' main concerns, 150
elitism, 122
pro-ana commandments, 124, 129
should be regulated, 132, 146–151
should not be regulated, 152–156
ANAD. See National Association of Anorexia Nervosa and Associated Disorders (ANAD)
Andersen, Arnold, 14
Anorexia, 34
    acceptance and commitment therapy, 185
    children, 68
    college women, 84–85
    diagnosis, 131
    disorder developmental model, 74
    family therapy, 159, 177–184
    genetics and, 71–72, 73, 74, 75, 78, 80–81, 108, 109
    involuntary treatment is justified, 161–170
    involuntary treatment mayn't be justified, 171–176
    mortality rates, 21, 24, 85, 121, 147, 162, 164, 173, 179
    personal narratives, 118, 120, 121–122, 128–129, 131–132, 133–134, 188
    prevalence, 34, 50, 94, 96, 100, 103, 122
    recovery, 72, 118, 121, 161, 162, 168, 173

voluntary treatment, 163
See also "Ana" websites
Anticonvulsant medications, 57
Antidepressant medications
    anorexia treatment, 165, 166
    binge eating disorder, 202
    bulimia treatment, 191–196
Appetite suppressants, 57, 83
Artistic expression
    poetry, 144
    thinspiration videos as misguided attempts, 140–145
    website artwork, 123, 144–145
Asian American women, 42–48
Assumptions of eating disorders, 88, 89–90
Athlete-model comparisons, 100
Athletes, competitive, 102–103, 142–143, 189
Attia, Evelyn, 123
Australia, and involuntary treatment, 163–164, 167
Avoidance, in disorders, 187, 190

B

Babies, feeding, 29, 113
Bacon, Linda, 59–65
Beat (Beating Eating Disorders), 148, 151
Beauty fads, 105
Beauty ideals. *See* "Ideal beauty"; Narrow definitions of beauty; "Real beauty" campaign (Dove)
Becker, Anne, 114–115
Behavior modeling, 109, 112–113
Behavioral therapy
    binge eating disorder, 49, 54–55, 56, 57, 197–202
    goals, 186
Bennett, Jessica, 93–99

Beverly Hills, 90210 (television program), 43, 115
Binge eating habits/disorder, 34, 49, 50, 53, 95
    behavioral therapy and structured eating plans, 49, 54–55, 56, 57, 197–202
    college women, 84–85, 198–199
    diagnosis, 51–53, 198
    linked to genetic and environmental factors, 107–115
    obesity links, 49–58
    personal narratives, 198–200, 202
    statistics, 50–51, 96, 198, 200
    See also Eating Disorder Not Otherwise Specified
Binge-purge cycle. *See* Bulimia
Bloggers
    Jeremy Gillitzer, 14
    recovery through blogging, 118, 179
Body image
    advertising/media and, 36–37, 82, 85–87, 94–96, 115, 125
    African Americans, 32, 35
    Asian Americans, 44–46
    children, 97–98
    definitions of eating disorders, 26, 29, 187, 192
    development of healthy, 73, 91, 92
    family issues, 75, 91
    historical perspectives, 98
    male ideals, 15, 30
    overweight, 52, 65
The Body Project (Brumberg), 96
Borderline personality disorder, 194
Borzekowski, Dina L.G., 122

Boughtwood, Desiree, 150
Boyer, Valérie, 143
Brain
    central nervous system and
        eating disorder genetics, 71–
        72, 80–81
    serotonin levels, 70, 71
Brisman, Judith, 68
Brody, Jane E., 197–202
Brooks, Gayle, 35
Brown, Janelle, 124
Brumberg, Joan Jacobs, 96, 98
Bulik, Cynthia M.
    binge eating linked to genetic
        and environmental factors,
        96–97, 107–115
    binge eating therapy, 53, 55–
        56, 201, 202
    media images and female
        body image, 95
Bulimia, 34
    acceptance and commitment
        therapy, 185
    antidepressant therapy, 191–
        196
    children, 68
    college women, 84–85
    deaths, 24, 138, 147
    diagnosis, 131
    disorder developmental
        model, 74
    exercise, 46, 183, 192
    genetics and, 72, 73, 74, 78,
        80–81, 108, 109
    personal narratives, 43, 46,
        47–48, 73, 112–113, 131,
        134, 136, 144–145
    prevalence, 34, 50, 96, 122
    "pro-mia" websites, dangers,
        120–126, 127, 146, 147–151
Byron, Tanya, 148–149, 151

C

Cancer risks, 63, 85
Cardiac arrhythmia, 21, 40, 169
Cardiac attacks and failure, 138–
    139, 169
Care and treatment. See Treatment
Cassell, Dana K., 36
Causes of eating disorders, 37–38
Cawley, Jane, 181
Celebrity culture
    icons/symbols, 87, 98
    weight focus, 83–84, 90, 115,
        141
Centers for Disease Control and
    Prevention (CDC), 60–61, 62, 94
Central nervous system, 80–81
Chang, Sand, 44, 45–46, 47
Cheng, Julia, 88–92
Children
    body image, 97–98, 125
    dieting, 28, 85
    eating disorders, 68–69, 85,
        125, 126
Cho, Margaret, 45
Christianity, 86–87
Clustering, eating disorders, 147
Coakley, Tedra, 32–41
Cognitive behavioral therapy. See
    Behavioral therapy
Cognitive impairments, 147, 172,
    174, 176, 177, 186
College students
    eating disorder-like behavior,
        84–85, 198–199
    eating habits, 89
    research over-focus, 45–46
Community belonging, 26, 30,
    86–87

Competence, anorexia patients,
162–164, 168, 170, 172–173, 174,
176
Complex (multifactorial) diseases,
77–78
Compulsory anorexia treatment.
See Involuntary anorexia treatment
Computer-based self-help programs, 55–56
Confessional poetry, 144
Congressional attention to eating
disorder issues, 20–25
Control issues
anorexia treatment and, 159,
163, 166, 171, 173–176, 177,
178–180, 181–184
reason for eating disorders,
37, 38, 47, 86, 87, 176, 187,
188
Council of Fashion Designers of
America (CFDA), 94, 99
Counseling, 40, 48
See also Treatment
Cox, Lauren, 120–126
Crawford, Cindy, 99
Cultural bias, overweight, 61, 65,
98–99
Cultural environments
eating habits and, 114–115
values of food, 46–47

D

Deardorff, Julie, 177–184
Deaths from eating disorders
anorexia, 14, 15, 85, 121, 162,
164, 168, 173, 174–175, 179
bulimia, 24, 138
denials of care, 22

Eating Disorder Not Otherwise Specified, 131
mortality rates and BMI, 65,
167, 169
as possible outcome/rates, 21,
24, 35, 132–133, 147
websites, 138–139
Deaths from overweight and obesity, 60–62
Definitions, eating disorders, 34
diagnosis criteria and subtleties, 46
too flexible, 26, 29
Dental problems, 40, 135
Depression
binge eating disorder and, 51,
53, 57, 198–199, 200–201
bulimia as, 193–194, 196
eating disorders and, 21, 165,
181
Developmental model for eating
disorders, 74
Diabetes
binge eating disorder and, 49,
51
medications, 63
risk of overweight, 85
Diagnosis
APA rulings, 51, 198
criteria, 45–46, 51, 55, 131
screening, 50, 52–53
*Diagnostic and Statistical Manual
of Mental Disorders* (DSM-IV),
51, 131
Diekman, Connie, 122
Diet aids and abuse, 43, 57, 83,
84, 102–103, 131, 192
Diet industry and programs, 27–
28, 30, 56, 83
Dieting
children, 28, 85

excessive, 26, 28, 108
  sports, 15, 100, 102–103
Digital culture, 143–144
Digital photo alteration, 95–96
Dilantin, 193
Disease/body fat correlations,
  63–64
Dopamine, 81
Dove, 90, 97–98
Doyle, Angela Celio, 159
Dreams, 189
Duration of eating disorders, 51

E

Eating Disorder Not Otherwise
  Specified, 46, 51, 131
    See also Binge eating habits/
      disorder
Eating Disorders Coalition for
  Research, Policy and Action, 25
Eating habits
  cultural shifts, 114–115
  eating plans, 197, 199–202
  excessive dieting, 26, 28, 108
  family environments and in-
    fluences, 28–29, 30, 73, 75,
    112–113
  fast food, 114, 183
  government recommenda-
    tions, 27
  healthy eating support, 21, 24
  males and eating disorders,
    15–16, 112–113
  Maudsley treatment for ano-
    rexia, 159, 178, 179, 181, 183
  naturally thin people, 88, 89
  selective eating disorder, 17,
    73
    See also Binge eating habits/
      disorder

Eating plans, and binge control,
  197–202
Economic drivers, fashion indus-
  try, 98–99, 101–102, 103
Education
  eating disorder prevention
    potential, 24, 155–156
  Internet safety, 148–149, 150,
    155–156
Edwards-Jones, Imogen, 98–99
Electrolyte imbalances, 40, 133,
  139, 169
Environmental factors
  binge eating and, 107–115
  interplay with genetic factors,
    73, 74, 75, 77, 78–79, 80,
    96–97, 107, 108, 110, 112–
    113, 115
  non-shared environmental
    experiences, 79–80, 110
Epidemiologic studies, 60, 62–63,
  108–113
Essence (periodical), 35, 36
Etcoff, Nancy, 97
Evans, Malcolm, 26–31
Exercise
  component of eating disorder,
    14, 34, 46, 73, 128, 181, 183,
    192
  means to health, 58
  means to perfect body, 87
Experiential avoidance, 187, 190
Extended family, 182
    See also Genetics and eating
      disorders

F

Family-based/Maudsley style anorexia treatment, 159, 177–184

Family influences. *See* Genetics and eating disorders; Guardianship; Parental control, anorexia treatment; Parental influence, eating disorders; Parental pressure; Parental support
Family meals, 181, 183
Fashion fads, 105
Fashion industry
    economics, 98–99, 101–102, 103
    promotes eating disorders, 93–99
    shouldn't be held responsible for eating disorders, 100–106
    thinness ideals, 15, 38, 83, 90, 93–99, *97*, 114
    See also Media images; Models
Fashion models. *See* Models
Fashion Week (New York City), 94, *97*, 99, 101
Fast food, 114, 134, 183
Feminism, 105–106
Fijians, 114–115
Fitness desires, 85
Fitness tests, 64
Fitzgibbon, Marian L., 34
Flegal, Katherine, 62
Fluoxetine, 192
Food allergies, 29
Food in culture, 46–47, 114–115
Food industry, 27, 29, 86
Food labels, 29
Food obsessions, 68, 86, 179
Force-feeding, as anorexia treatment, 159, 161, 163, 165–166, 167, 168, 173–174
France, proposed pro-ana sites ban, 143, 149, 153–154

Fraternal twins, 76, 78, 80, 110–111
Freeman, Michael, 104

G

Gallucci, Jaclyn, 127–139
Genetic disorders, 80, 109
Genetics and depression, 72, 193, 194, 196
Genetics and eating disorders
    binge eating, 107–115
    eating disorders developmental model, *74*
    genetics may not play significant role, 76–81
    genetics play significant role, 70–75, 108, 109, 179–180
    interplay: genes and environment, 73, 74, 75, 77, 78–79, 80, 96–97, 107, 108, 110, 112–113, 115
    parent and child disorders, 68
Germany, and involuntary treatment, 164–166, 168
Gillitzer, Jeremy, 14
Giordano, Simona, 76–81
Gitlin, Michael J., 191–196
Gleaves, David H., 36
Globalization
    eating disorders, 23, 28
    food industry, 27, 114
Glück, Louise, 144
Grandparents, 182
Group identity, 26, 30, 86, 87
Guardianship, 164–165, 166, 169, 172

H

Hair loss, 40, 128
Halmi, Katherine, 200, 201

Halse, Christine, 150

Harris, Shannette, 35

Health consequences and side effects. *See* Medical consequences and side effects

Health insurance coverage, 22–23, 25

Heart attacks and failure, 138–139, 169, 173

Heart disease
eating disorders causes, 40, 49, 51
medication risks, 64
risk of overweight, 85

Heffernan, Virginia, 140–145

Hersh, Carolyn, 36, 37

Herzog, David, 125

Hilton, Lisa, 100–106

Honey, Anne, 150

Hospitalization rates
anorexics, 164, 167
males, 15
See also Treatment

Hudson, James I., 15, 50, 51, 52, 56, 57

Human Genome Project, 111

I

"Ideal beauty"
advertising and, 36–37, 38
African American ideals, 32, 35
Asian American ideals, 42, 44
global differences and trends, 23
male bodies, 15
narrowly defined, 38, 84, 90–91, 97
"real beauty" movement, 88, 90, 97–98

thinness, 15, 23, 35, 36, 42, 44–45, 82–87, 114

Identical twins, 76, 78–79, 80, 109–110

Impulse control problems, 74

Infant feeding, 29, 113

Insel, Thomas R., 71–72

Insurance coverage eating disorders, 22–23, 55

Intensive care treatment, 165

Internet. *See* Bloggers; Internet usage and safety, children and teens; Websites

Internet usage and safety, children and teens, 124–126, 137–138, 146, 147, 148–151

Interpersonal therapy, 56

Involuntary anorexia treatment
is justified, 161–170
legal ethics, 168, 169–170, 172–173, 174
may not justified in some cases, 171–176
recovered patients' outcomes and attitudes, 162, 175
studies described, 164–168
See also Maudsley (family-based) anorexia treatment

IQ, 112

IV feeding. *See* Tube- and IV-feeding, as anorexia treatment

J

Jasper, Karin, 86

Jockeys, 102–103

Johnson, Craig, 72

Journal of the American Medical Association (JAMA), 60–61, 62

K

Kandel, Johanna S., 70–75, 121, 126
Kater, Kathy, 185–190
Kaye, Walter, 72, 73, 179–180
Kolb, Steven, 99
Koreans and Korean Americans, 44–45, 46, 47–48

L

Lagerfeld, Karl, 102
Le Grange, Daniel, 180–181, 182
Learning environments, 112
Lee, Szu-Hui, 48
Legal guardianship, 164–165, 166, 169, 172
Lelwica, Michelle M., 82–87
Life expectancy, overweight vs. normal weight, 60, 62–63
Lifestyle choice, anorexia spun as, 144, 147, 150, 153
Liver damage, 40
Loeb, Katharine, 181
Low, Elaine, 42–48
Low blood pressure, 39
Lowe, Daisy, 102

M

Males
    anorexia, 183
    "bigspiration" videos, 142–143
    binge eating disorder, 51
    eating disorder deaths, 14
    eating disorders prevalence, 15, 16, 122, 180
    overlooked in issue, 14–16
    sharing stories, 14, 183
    sports dieting, 15, 100, 102–103
    weight loss reasoning, 15–16
Maudsley (family-based) anorexia treatment, 159, 177–184
Media images
    airbrushing and manipulation, 95–96, 125
    fashion industry not responsible for eating disorders, 100–106
    fashion industry promotes eating disorders, 93–99
    thinness backlash, 94
    thinness obsession and harms, 15, 36–37, 38, 82, 83–87, 90, 98, 104, 114
    See also Advertising; Fashion industry
Medical consequences and side effects, 21, 24–25, 39–40, 101, 128, 131, 135, 147, 169
Medical treatment. *See* Antidepressant medications; Treatment
Medication. *See* Antidepressant medications
Men. *See* Males
Menstruation, 39, 131
Mental competence, anorexia patients, 162–164, 170, 172–173, 174, 176
Mental Health Act of New South Wales (1990), 163–164, 167
Mental problems. *See* Psychological problems
Meyer, Joanne M., 74
MiAna Land (website), 133
Mindfulness, 187, 188–189
Minorities and obesity, 64

Minority women
    African Americans, 32–41
    Asian Americans, 42–48
    disorder prevalence, 16, 33, 36, 85
Mitchell, James E., 54
Modeling, behavior, 112–113
Models
    curvy bodies, 99, 102
    deaths, 14, 15
    Dove's Campaign for Real Beauty, 90
    image manipulation and airbrushing, 95–96, 125
    media images, 83, 87, 90, 93, 94–99
    personal stories, 14, 98, 102
    as professional/disciplined, 100, 101–103
    thinness backlash, 94, 99
    thinness rate trends, 93, 95, 97, 104, 114
    thinspiration, 120, 122, 129, 140
    See also Fashion industry
Mok, Teresa, 44, 46
Monoamine oxidase inhibitors, 192, 195–196
Moore, Stephanie, 118
Mortality. See Deaths from eating disorders
Moss, Kate, 104
Multifactorial diseases, 77–78
Muscular dystrophy, 80

N

Narrow definitions of beauty, 38, 84, 90–91, 97
Natenshon, Abigail H., 68

National Association of Anorexia Nervosa and Associated Disorders (ANAD), 22, 36, 40, 41, 121, 148
National Eating Disorders Association (NEDA), 37–38, 40, 130, 148
National Institute of Mental Health, 71
Neurotransmitters, 70, 71, 80–81
Nichter, Mimi, 91
Non-shared environmental experiences, 79–80, 110
Normalization, by media, of unhealthy behaviors, 86
Nutritional needs
    education, 24, 40, 53–54
    selective eating disorder and, 17

O

Obesity
    binge eating disorder links, 49–58, 198–199, 200
    deaths, 60, 61–62
    discrimination, 65
    epidemic is myth that promotes unhealthy weight loss, 59–65
    ethnic minorities, 64
    genetics and, 108
    medications, 64
    national increases and "epidemics," 27, 94, 100, 103, 114
Obsession, food, 68, 86, 179
Oligogenic diseases, 77
Opioids, 81
Osteoporosis, 39

Otis, Carré, 98
Owens, Jemima, 118

P

Parental control, anorexia treatment, 159, 172, 177, 178–184
See also Guardianship
Parental influence, eating disorders, 68, 108–109, 112–113
Parental pressure, 37, 45, 47, 91
Parental support, 125–126, 151, 159, 178–179, 181, 183
Paul, T., 164, 168–169
Peer pressure, 147
Perfectionism, 37, 73, 84, 87, 97, 179–180
Photo alteration, 95–96, 125
Physical abilities, 91, 92
"Picky" eating. *See* Selective eating disorder
Plath, Sylvia, 144
Poetry, 144
Polygenic diseases, 77
Prevalence, eating disorders
    children, 85
    global trends, 23, 28, 40–41
    men, 15, 16, 122, 180
    minority women, 16, 33, 36, 85
    totals, 21, 43, 50, 96, 180, 198
    types, 34, 46, 50, 54, 94, 96, 103, 122, 198
    women, 43, 84–85, 103, 122, 180
Prevention
    healthy eating education/ support, 21, 24
    research funding support, 24–25
    talk therapy, 47–48

Pro-anorexia websites. *See* "Ana" websites
Psychological problems
    cultural stigmas, 42, 47, 48
    depression, 193–194, 196, 198–199, 200–201
    eating disorder associations, 21, 25, 37, 38, 51, 53, 144, 193–194, 199, 200–201
    eating disorder classifications, 22, 35, 43, 71–73, 121, 123, 163–164, 167–168
    genetics and, 109, 193, 194, 196
    hospitalization, 164, 166, 167
    mental capacity determinations, 162–164, 168, 172
Public health threats
    binge eating disorder, 51
    as distorted, 26–31
    obesity portrayals, 60–63
    as significant, 20–25

R

Ranalli, Rina, 178, 179, 181, 183, 184
Rathner, Günther, 175
Ravin, Sarah, 159
Re-feeding therapy. *See* Maudsley (family-based) anorexia treatment
"Real beauty" campaign (Dove), 88, 90, 97–98
Relapses
    accounts, 14, 198
    fears, 118
    possibilities, 57, 166, 186, 195
    treatment coverage limits, 22–23
Religion, 86–87, 129

Research bias, racial, 44, 45–46
Research errors, 60
Research funding, 24–25
Research surveys, 50–51, 54
Right to refuse treatment. *See* Mental competence, anorexia patients
Rituals, 68, 87, 129, 137, 186
Robb, Adelaide, 15–16
Rosen, David, 15
Royal College of Psychiatrists, 146–151
Rumney, Avis, 171–176
Runway models, 94, 97, 99
  See also Models

S

Safer Children in a Digital World (report), 148–149, 151
Sasha (model), 102
Schmidt, U., 176
Schnur, Nate and Jacqui, 183
Schurman, Jennifer, 184
Secret-keeping, 48, 131, 134
Sedentary vs. active lifestyles, 63–64, 155
Selective eating disorder, 17, 73
Selective serotonin reuptake inhibitors, 57
Self-destructive behaviors, 68
Self-esteem
  development of healthy, 73
  low esteem as eating disorder risk, 38, 44, 46, 74
  low self esteem, barrier creation, 97–98
  overweight, 52
  See also Body image

Self-help
  binge eating disorder, 49, 55–56, 199–200
  diet industry, 83
Self-portraits, 128, 140, 141
Selis, Sara, 49–58
Senate Committee on Health, Education, Labor and Pensions, 20–25
Serotonin levels, 70, 71, 81
Setliff, Stephanie, 124–125
Sexton, Anne, 144
Siblings, 182
Side effects. *See* Deaths from eating disorders; Medical consequences and side effects
Sim, Leslie, 126
Smith, Anna Nicole, 99
Social contagion, 147
Socioeconomic status and obesity, 64
South Carolina Department of Mental Health, 103
Spelt, Jeanine R., 74
Spiritual needs, 86–87
Stereotypes
  eating disorders as female issue, 16
  eating disorders as white issue, 32, 33, 34–35, 43–44, 45–46
  thin women, 88, 89–90
Stolley, Melinda R., 34
Stone, Lara, 102
Strength, physical, 91, 92
Stress management, 68, 187, 188, 194–195, 202
  See also Control issues
Striegel-Moore, Ruth, 34, 35, 52, 53, 55, 57–58

Sugar-free foods, 86

Suicide

    Asian American women, 48

    eating disorder groups and, 136–137

    eating disorder links, 21, 169, 173

    reasoning/ideation, 174, 199

Support groups, 32, 40–41

    families discussed, 73

    online, 127, 129–131, 134–137, 151

T

Tabloid news, 84

Tay-Sachs disease, 80

Teasing, 89, 91

Tegretol, 193

Television, 43–44, 115, 137

Therapy. *See* Behavioral therapy; Treatment

Thiel, A., 164, 168–169

Thiels, Cornelia, 161–170

Thierer, Adam, 152–156

Thinness

    Asian Americans/Asians, 42, 44–45

    backlash and changing opinions, 94, 99

    cultural values/obsession, 23, 36–37, 38, 82–87, 90, 93, 104, 114

    models are professional/disciplined, 100, 101–103

    models growing thinner, 15, 93, 95, 104

    some perceptions are unfair and harmful, 88–92

"Thinspiration"

    disorder blogging, photos, and discussion, 118, 120, 121, 122, 128, 129, 132

    Web videos, 140–145

    See also "Ana" websites

Tiller, J., 167–168, 176

Tooth decay, 40, 135

Trazodone, 192

Treasure, J., 176

Treatment, 40–41

    access challenges, 22–23, 52, 55

    anorexia, 72, 123, 159, 161–170, 171–176, 177–184

    binge eating disorder, 49, 53–58

    impaired cognitive functioning and, 147, 172, 174, 176, 177, 186

    involuntary, ethics issues, 161–170, 171–176

    Maudsley (family-based) method, 159, 177–184

    minorities' lack of treatment, 32, 34–35, 42, 48

    pro-ana websites and, 123–125, 144, 147–148

    psychiatric treatment challenges, 166, 175

    refusal, 123, 132–133, 144, 147, 163, 164, 165, 166, 167–168, 171, 172, 174, 178, 180

    research, 162, 164–170, 176

    self-help, 49, 55–56, 199–200

    See also Involuntary anorexia treatment

Trebay, Guy, 15

Troscianko, Emily, 179

Tube- and IV-feeding, as anorexia treatment, 161, 163, 165–166, 167, 168, 171, 174

Twiggy (model), 114
Twin studies, 72–73, 76, 78–79, 80, 107, 109–111

U

UK Council for Child Internet Safety, 149, 150
United Kingdom, and involuntary treatment, 164, 166, 174
United States, and involuntary treatment, 164, 168
US Senate Committee on Health, Education, Labor and Pensions, 20–25

V

Videos, websites, 123, 140–145
Voluntary anorexia treatment, 163
  See also Involuntary anorexia treatment
von Fürstenberg, Diane, 94

W

Wadden, Thomas, 202
Walsh, B. Timothy, 123, 200–201
Warning signs, for eating disorders, 39
Websites
  main concerns of pro-ana sites, 150

pro-ana and -mia sites are dangerous, 120–126, 129
pro-ana elitism, 122
pro-ana sites should be regulated, 132, 146–151
pro-ana sites should not be regulated, 152–156
support in recovery, 118, 120, 123, 127–139
thinspiration videos, 140–145
  See also Bloggers
Weight discrimination, 59, 65
Weight Foundation, 26
Weight gain challenges (non-disordered eating), 89, 90
Weight restrictions, sports, 15, 102–103
Western culture exports. *See* Globalization
White women
  eating disorder research limitations, 44, 45–46
  eating disorder stereotypes, 32, 33, 34–35, 43–44
  media images, and lack of diversity, 43–44, 97, 115
Wright, Snowden, 16

Y

Yager, Joel, 173, 174, 201
YouTube videos, 143, 144–145